DEDICATION:

This guide was written by Georgina Bottomley and Andrew Bruff.

Georgina Bottomley is an English teacher from Dorset with 13 years of teaching experience. She is a happily married mother of two.

Georgina Bottomley would like to thank Andrew Bruff for his valuable time and expert advice when proofreading the final draft of this book and Neil Bottomley for his ongoing support.

Andrew Bruff is a pioneer in online education. A sought-after school consultant and former Head of English, his teaching videos on YouTube have been viewed over 40 million times around the world.

Andrew Bruff would like to thank the following, who gave permission for their work to be used in this guide: Manfred Pfister, Maggie B. Gale, BBC Bitesize, Tom Briars-Delve. He would also like to thank Sam Perkins, who designed the front cover of this eBook.

IMPORTANT NOTE:

This guide is not endorsed by, or affiliated with, any exam boards. The writers are simply two experienced English teachers who are using their skills and expertise to help students.

BIBLIOGRAPHY:

Quotations from AN INSEPCTOR CALLS AND OTHER PLAYS by J. B. Priestley (these plays first published by William Heineman 1948-50, first published by Penguin Books 1969, Penguin Classics 2000). 'An Inspector Calls' copyright 1947 by J. B. Priestley are reproduced by permission of Penguin Books Ltd.

Gale, Maggie, J.B. Priestley (Routledge, 2008).

Hands, Thora, Drinking in Victorian and Edwardian Britain – Beyond the Spectre of the Drunkard (2018) Licensed under Creative Commons.

Pfister, Manfred, The Theory and Analysis of Drama (Cambridge: Cambridge University Press, 1991) .

Priestley, J.B, Theatre Outlook (Nicholson & Watson, 1947).

FREE GIFT:

As a thank you for buying this book, we would like to give you the eBook edition free of charge. Simply email proof of purchase to info@mrbruff.com to claim your free gift.

Contents

J. B. Priestley

J. B. Priestley (John Boynton Priestley) was born in Bradford, Yorkshire, in September 1894. His parents were middle class, and his surroundings were probably not too dissimilar to the town of Brumley where the Birling family from the play live.

At the age of sixteen, Priestley left school to work as a clerk in a wool office before joining the British Army at the start of the First World War; he served on the Western Front and took part in the Battle of Loos. He was wounded in 1916, and some of his work reflects on his war experiences.

In 1919, Priestley went to Cambridge University and then moved to London to be a writer. Despite producing novels, essays and articles, Priestley is now primarily known as a playwright. Much of his writing includes his strong political beliefs and his hatred of lies and hypocrisy. We see evidence of this when he explores the inequalities in society in 'An Inspector Calls'.

In 1942, Priestley helped to set up the Common Wealth Party, a new socialist political party that believed in public ownership of land and a stronger emphasis on democracy. As a socialist, Priestley believed that we are all part of the same society and should therefore share any wealth and benefits. He thought it was essential that we all contribute to society rather than just take from it. In 1945, two thirds of the Common Wealth Party joined the Labour Party, and the Common Wealth Party was dissolved in 1993.

During the Second World War, Priestley had a weekly slot on BBC Radio. Eventually, his broadcasts were cancelled, probably due to his criticism of the government of the time. Winston Churchill's Conservative cabinet believed his messages to be too left wing. It is possible that his broadcasts helped influence people to accept his ideas and, in turn, contributed to the Labour Party's win in the 1945 General Election. The character of Inspector Goole in 'An Inspector Calls' is the socialist voice of Priestley.

Having lived through two world wars, Priestley believed that war should be avoided. The only way this could happen would be for countries to have a greater respect for one another. For this reason, Priestley was involved in the early movement for a United Nations.

Priestley studied the concept of time, including Ouspensky's theory, which suggests that when we die, we restart our lives if we have failed to learn from any mistakes made in that lifetime. He also studied Dunne's theory, which again focuses on learning from mistakes. This theory proposes that we have all been given the ability to look forward in time so that we can avoid errors before we make them (as well as learning from mistakes in our past). The idea of learning from your mistakes is certainly a key idea in 'An Inspector Calls'.

J. B. Priestley continued writing until a few years before his death in 1984.

Social and Historical Context: Important Events in Priestley's Life

Key Dates
1894
Priestley is born.

1895
'The Time Machine' is written by H.G. Wells, a socialist who supported the suffragettes and believed (like Priestley) that hope for the future could come from education and learning through history.

1903
The Women's Social and Political Union is founded by Emmeline Pankhurst, aiming to help women gain the right to vote.

1904
There is a dramatic increase in the number of people who are receiving charitable aid.
3000 London cabbies go on strike.

1905
500 striking workers are shot by the Tsar's troops in Russia.

1908
2000 cotton workers go on strike in England.
200,000 women take part in a suffragette demonstration in London.

1912
The 'unsinkable' Titanic sinks after hitting an iceberg. 1912 is the year in which 'An Inspector Calls' is set.

1913
Emily Davison dies trying to stop the King's horse in the Derby.

1914
Start of the First World War.
Priestley serves in France in the trenches.
Builders and miners go on strike.

1918
The First World War ends.
Women over the age of 30 with minimum property qualifications can vote for the first time in the UK.

1926
The General Strike occurs: workers protest against unemployment and the treatment of miners.

1928
All women over the age of 21 are given the vote.

1939
The Second World War starts.
The Holocaust starts.

1942
The idea of the Welfare State is proposed.

1945

The Second World War ends.

Priestley writes 'An Inspector Calls'.

Written in 1945 but set in 1912

In 1912 when the play is set, the ruling classes, keen to stay in power, saw no need for change. The Birlings, a wealthy family, represent others of a similar status; they are heavily criticised by Priestley in the play (via the inspector), as they initially take no responsibility for their actions and the effect they have on others.

An audience at the time (from 1945 to the present day) would have been aware through Priestley's use of dramatic irony that a family such as the Birlings would soon hear about the sinking of the Titanic. There would then be two world wars.

1912	1945
'An Inspector Calls' is set in 1912.	'An Inspector Calls' was written in 1945.
World War I is yet to start. Birling's view that 'The Germans don't want war' is known to be incorrect by all audience members, as the play was first performed in 1945 (Moscow) and 1946 (London).	World War II ended on the 8th May 1945. British audiences were recovering from nearly six years of warfare, danger and uncertainty.
The Titanic was in production but had not begun its ill-fated maiden voyage.	Audiences knew that the Titanic sank in 1912.
There was a patriarchal society—men were seen as more powerful than women. Working-class women were regarded as cheap labour. Women were expected to marry and have children. If men could afford to support their wives, married women were not expected to work. More affluent women employed servants to do the housework and to share the responsibility of looking after the children.	As a result of the wars and the suffragette movement, women were more valued in society.
The ruling classes saw no need to change their position. There was a strong divide between the upper and lower classes.	There was a great desire for social change and, primarily as a result of the wars, there were fewer divisions between classes.

Having witnessed these wars, Priestley, questions what kind of society people were fighting to save. The very idea of society suggests a group of people working together and looking out for one another: in Priestley's opinion, social responsibility is vital. By reminding his audience of pre-war characters, Priestley wants his audiences to consider the nature of the post-war society they were building.

The attitude of the Birlings and the way they are so quick to dismiss any involvement with the unpleasantness of Eva's suicide would, no doubt, resonate with an audience who had lived through the consequences of such complacency and ignorance.

An audience in the mid-1940s would still have been deprived of many of the luxuries that the Birlings enjoy at the beginning of the play. Rationing continued into the 1950s, so the wealthy Birlings might be regarded as materialistic and superficial.

Priestley may well have set his play in 1912 because it started a time of great change. In the period between 1912 and 1945, class and gender differences were becoming less pronounced. There was hope for a better future if young people could be educated to take responsibility for their actions and their treatment of others.

The Setting – Brumley

'An Inspector Calls' is set in the fictitious industrial city of Brumley. We learn through the course of the play that it has a police force with its own constable and a lord mayor (a position which was once held by Mr Birling). The city was visited two years ago by royalty, which signifies that it is a thriving and important city. Priestley's own home town of Bradford in Yorkshire is a similar industrial city, which probably had many similar features to Brumley.

The existence of Brumley Women's Charity Organisation suggests that there is an underclass of poor and desperate women. Eva Smith represents these women.

Act 1: A Summary

The play opens with Mr and Mrs Birling, Sheila Birling, Eric Birling and Gerald Croft finishing dinner and celebrating the engagement of Sheila to Gerald. The port is passed around, and Mr Birling makes a speech about how happy he is with the engagement of his daughter Sheila to Gerald Croft. Surprisingly, he does not talk about love and happiness. Instead, he expresses the hope that Sheila's marriage to Gerald will create an opportunity to improve Mr Birling's business prospects. Gerald is a man whose parents own an even more successful company than Birling and Co., and Mr Birling hopes that one day, they will work together. Mr Birling presents the engagement almost as a business deal. He seems concerned that he does not have the same kind of family connections as Gerald. Therefore, Mr Birling has to rely on money that he has made rather than an inheritance.

Mr Birling seems very proud of his standing in society and frequently reminds everyone of his achievement of being a Lord Mayor and his hope of a knighthood. His mention of the knighthood is significant, as this is an award given for services to the community. However, Priestley seems to be criticising Mr Birling and his actions: we later learn that he does not support the notion of community at all.

After the toast, Gerald gives Sheila an engagement ring, and it is only at this point that she says she feels engaged; it is as if she needs the symbol of the ring to truly see herself as Gerald's fiancée. This makes Sheila seem rather superficial. Despite agreeing to the engagement, Sheila has some suspicions about Gerald and his absences the previous summer. This builds tension and foreshadows the conflict to come when we later learn exactly where Gerald was.

Mr Birling describes the Titanic as 'unsinkable' and asserts that the 'Germans don't want war.' A contemporary audience will be well aware that Mr Birling is very much mistaken. Those living in Britain in 1912 (as the Birlings are) would soon be experiencing the sinking of the Titanic, two world wars and a number of strikes and unrest. When Mr Birling follows these statements with comments about 'community and all that nonsense', the audience is likely to think that he is again wrong. It is at this point that Priestley begins to achieve his aim—to make the audience aware that community is in fact far from 'nonsense'. Priestley believed a sense of community was essential if society was to become a caring place where people could live happily, no matter what their social status.

Mrs Birling plays little part in these early conversations, reinforcing her description as 'cold' from the stage directions. The first part of the play is chiefly focused on Mr Birling, his lifestyle and opinions.

The stage directions announce the arrival of Inspector Goole with a 'sharp ring'. It is almost as if the doorbell has been personified and is angrily interrupting Mr Birling's capitalist views. Edna, the parlour maid, shows the inspector in with Mr Birling again emphasises his standing in society, including having previously been Lord Mayor. The inspector is unimpressed by Mr Birling's claims about his position. He explains that he is there to investigate the death of a young lady who has committed suicide by drinking disinfectant. He is direct with his words from the start, and the nature of the young lady's death is shocking. This would surely gain the sympathy of the audience, as well as that of the characters on stage at the time.

As inspector Goole arrives, the stage directions at the start of Act 1 state that the lighting should change from 'pink and intimate' to 'brighter and harder'. It is as if he has arrived to remove the rose-tinted spectacles from the Birling family, put them under a spotlight and shed light on their true nature.

The inspector is completely focused on the task at hand and sets to work questioning Mr Birling, whose involvement started the 'chain of events' that led to Eva Smith's death. Mr Birling is told the victim's name and shown a photograph. The audience never gets to see the photograph, and the inspector only ever shows it to one character at a time. For this reason, it is not clear whether or not they are all being shown the same picture.

Mr Birling soon remembers that Eva was an employee at his factory and admits he sacked her due to her involvement in strike action over wages. He says she was one of the ring-leaders, and he still believes he was right to fire her, even though she was a hard-working employee who was about to be promoted. We see a change in Mr Birling's mood at this point. He is no longer the relaxed, bragging character from the opening of the play. He is now forced to explain and defend the decisions he made. It is clear that he is driven chiefly by money and status: he cares little for the lives of those affected by his actions. Mr Birling is depicted as a caricature of a typical capitalist businessman of the time: heartless and ruthless, concerned only with himself and his wealth. We, the audience, are likely to find it hard to sympathise with his opinions.

The inspector soon directs his attention to Sheila Birling, who re-enters the dining room. Eric starts to comment on the proceedings, recognising that his father's actions may have begun the series of events that resulted in Eva Smith's suicide. Gerald, however, sides with Mr Birling, and he cannot see how sacking Eva from the factory could result in the eventual tragic outcome.

Inspector Goole gradually reveals more about Eva's life. After she was sacked from Birling and Co., she ended up unemployed for two months. She had no parents, relatives or friends to help her, and soon became desperate. It was then that she secured a job at Milwards Department Store where she was to meet Sheila.

Hearing what happened to Eva upsets Sheila far more than her father, but she still does not recognise Eva's name. The inspector shows her a photograph; the audience cannot be sure that it is the same picture that was shown to Mr Birling earlier, or whether this is a different woman. Nevertheless, Sheila is immediately upset. Mr Birling leaves the room to look for his wife. Gerald tries to look at the picture, but the inspector, always controlling the situation, tells him he must wait.

We learn that Eva was happy in her job at Milwards until a valuable customer complained about her and she was consequently sacked. That customer turns out to be Sheila Birling. Sheila had tried a dress on that had not suited her and, whilst she was looking in the mirror, she saw Eva smiling at the shop assistant, Miss Francis. This had infuriated Sheila. Earlier, when fetching the dress for Sheila, Eva had held the dress up to herself. Sheila explains that it had suited Eva Smith. Sheila had become jealous when she had tried on the dress, which did not look as good on her as it did held up against Eva. Sheila believed the smile Eva had given the assistant was mocking her. Furious, Sheila had complained to the manager. The store did not want to lose the business of the Birling family, so sacked Eva.

Unlike her father, Sheila shows remorse for her actions. The stage directions explain that she looks 'as if she's been crying'. She later states 'I behaved badly too.' Priestley uses Sheila's character to demonstrate that young people can learn the lesson of social responsibility, and that there is hope for the future and Priestley's socialist ideas.

Next, the inspector explains how, after losing her job at Milwards, Eva Smith changed her name to Daisy Renton. Gerald reacts immediately when he hears this name, and it is clear that he is next in the firing line although the details of his involvement are not actually revealed until Act 2. There is then a reminder from earlier in the play that the previous summer, Sheila had not seen much of Gerald and had become suspicious about his whereabouts. He admits to Sheila that he had a relationship with Eva/Daisy, but that it ended sixth months ago. Therefore, he thinks it had no bearing on her suicide. The act ends with Gerald believing that he can keep his affair with Daisy a secret from the inspector, but Sheila recognises that this is not possible.

Quick Quiz: Act 1

1. What are the Birling family celebrating at the very start of the play?

2. Why is Mr Birling happy about his daughter's situation?

3. Name two false predictions that Mr Birling makes about historical events.

4. Which word describes Mrs Birling early in the play?

5. How is the inspector's arrival announced?

6. How does the inspector say Eva Smith committed suicide?

7. How did Mr Birling meet Eva Smith?

8. Where does Sheila meet Eva?

9. Which item of clothing looked better on Eva than on Sheila?

10. What does Eva change her name to after being sacked from Milwards, according to the inspector?

Act 2: A Summary

Act 2 begins in the same way that Act 1 ends, with the inspector repeating his question, 'Well?'. The question is aimed at Gerald.

Gerald tries to stop Sheila from hearing the details, claiming that she has suffered enough upset already, but she insists on staying. At the time the play is set, women were thought of as delicate, fragile creatures who should be protected. Sheila proves that they can withstand traumatic events and can learn from their mistakes—a point on gender equality that Priestley was trying to raise whilst writing the play. After all, Eva had not been spared any upset or pain in the years leading up to her death. The inspector highlights the idea of shared responsibility: if Sheila is sent away, she will be alone with her feelings of guilt. She is allowed to stay.

Mrs Birling notes how upset Sheila is by the revelations. When talking about learning from their mistakes and accepting responsibility, the inspector comments on how 'young ones' are 'more impressionable'.

Before the full story of Gerald's relationship with Eva is revealed, Mrs Birling's relationship with Eric is explored. She does not want to listen to the suggestions that Eric drinks too much; even Gerald knows more about her son than she does. The distance in the mother-son relationship prepares us for the end of the act when Mrs Birling inadvertently tells the inspector that the father of Eva's child is to blame for the young woman's desperate situation. Mrs Birling does not realise at the time that she is in fact blaming her own son.

Mr Birling then encourages the inspector to question Eric, so that his son can get it over with and go to bed. The inspector refuses, again ensuring his complete control over the situation and the order of events. Sheila clearly recognises the power of the inspector and how they really are at his mercy. Mr and Mrs Birling are less keen to see this, and they try to regain control wherever they see the opportunity.

The attention then returns to Gerald, who is forced to tell the story of his contribution to the tragic 'chain of events' that led to the demise of Eva. After a brief moment trying to deny his involvement again, Gerald admits that he met her in the bar at the Palace Variety Theatre. This is a place known to be the haunt of prostitutes, but he says that Daisy (as he knew her) looked different to those girls. She had a youthful, innocent look which made her stand out. Eric later reveals that he also met Eva in the same bar and also noticed how she stood out in comparison to the other women there.

Gerald explains that Daisy was being harassed by Alderman Meggarty, and he says he wanted to help her. Gerald took Daisy to the County Hotel where they had a drink and talked. Gerald asked Daisy lots of questions about her background and learned of her sacking from both Birling and Co. and Milwards, although she was vague about the actual company names. He also saw that she was struggling for money and had not eaten, so he arranged for some food to be brought to her.

Two nights later, Gerald arranged to meet Eva again. He found her somewhere to live and began a relationship with her. He insists that he did not arrange the accommodation just to have an affair with her.

When questioned about the closeness of their relationship, Gerald is not clear about whether or not he was in love with Eva. He suggests that her feelings for him were stronger than his towards her. It was only when he had to go away on business that Gerald broke up with her. He gave her some money to ensure she could manage on her own for a while. He did not know exactly what her plans were, but his belief that she left Brumley is confirmed by Inspector Goole—according to her diary, Eva went to the seaside to think of Gerald and remember the positive aspects of the relationship.

At this point, Sheila returns Gerald's engagement ring. Both Sheila and Gerald regret their actions and, whilst she recognises that he was trying to help Daisy, Sheila does not feel their relationship is in the same place as it was at the start of the evening. Gerald leaves the house and goes for a walk.

Gerald is never shown a photograph of Eva, but Mrs Birling is. She says she does not recognise the girl in the picture. The inspector insists that she must know the girl, and Mr Birling interrupts to demand an apology. When Mr Birling yet again tries to use his social standing to exert authority over the inspector, he is sharply reminded that those with authority have responsibilities as well as privileges. Inspector Goole voices Priestley's key message of social responsibility at every opportunity.

Sheila accepts the need for them all to admit their guilt. She recaps the 'chain of events' so far: Eva's sacking from Birling and Company, her sacking from Milwards and her relationship with Gerald, which came to an end. She advises her mother to confess to her role. The inspector's interrogation of Mrs Birling begins.

Mrs Birling has a similar approach to the situation as her husband, failing to take any responsibility for her actions. Now a desperate, pregnant, penniless woman, Eva went to the Brumley Women's Charity Organisation. In the early 1900s, it was not socially acceptable for unmarried women to have children, so her pregnancy would certainly have been frowned upon. Eva, knowing this was the case, pretended that she was married when she asked for help. Since the father of her baby was Eric, she called herself Mrs Birling, having no idea that the woman from whom she was seeking help was actually his mother.

The real Mrs Birling assumed that Eva was rudely copying her name. She took offence and refused her help. Her reaction could be compared to that of Sheila. They both took offence to something that Eva did; both Birlings overreacted, making Eva's terrible situation even worse. Sheila, uncaring at the time, left her jobless; Mrs Birling left her pregnant, alone, penniless and later suicidal.

During the inspector's interrogation, Mrs Birling refuses to accept any responsibility for her actions. In doing so, she unwittingly accuses her own son, telling Goole to 'Go and look for the father of the child. It's his responsibility'.

The inspector emphasises how Mrs Birling's refusal of help really did affect Eva badly. She had been left alone, poor and only needing advice and some money, but Mrs Birling had not been willing to offer her anything, despite having children of her own.

Even though she clearly understands the situation, Mrs Birling shows no remorse whatsoever. Almost predictably by this stage, Mr Birling is more worried about the effect the revelations might have on his reputation if the press finds out. He is, after all, expecting a knighthood, and he does not want anything to harm his chances of receiving one. Both Mr and Mrs Birling appear to be very selfish characters whose aim is only to protect themselves and their social status.

Mrs Birling attempts to deflect the attention from herself onto the other family members, suggesting it was her husband and daughter who forced Eva into unemployment that may have started the 'chain of events' that ended in such a sad and tragic way. Mrs Birling can be likened to her husband in the play. Neither accepts any responsibility for their actions; neither learns the lesson of social responsibility. By showing them both acting in this way, Priestley highlights the need to focus on educating the younger generation because they are more 'impressionable' and able to change.

Quick Quiz: Act 2

1. Which character does the inspector start questioning at the start of Act 2?

2. Where did Gerald first meet Eva?

3. Why did Eva end up leaving Brumley? Where did she go?

4. Where did Mrs Birling meet Eva?

5. What did Eva call herself when she first met Mrs Birling?

6. Mrs Birling thought she was just being rude but why did Eva give herself the name 'Mrs Birling' when she went to the organisation for help?

7. Does Mrs Birling accept responsibility for her actions?

8. Who does Mrs Birling blame for the death of Eva Smith?

9. Which award does Mr Birling think he is due to receive? (He therefore does not want any negative attention from the press.)

10. Why didn't Eva take the money she had been offered by the father of her baby?

Answers

1. Gerald.
2. The bar in the Palace Variety Theatre.
3. To the seaside, to get over the failed relationship with Gerald.
4. At the Brumley Women's Charity Organisation.
5. She called herself 'Mrs Birling'.
6. She pretended she was married to Eric Birling, who had got her pregnant.
7. No
8. Eric, her own son (before realising he was the father of Eva's child).
9. A knighthood.
10. She realised it had been stolen (showing her good morals), in even a time of extreme difficulty.)

Act 3: A Summary

Act 3 picks up exactly where Act 2 leaves off, with Eric having arrived home. He acknowledges that it is pointless to try to keep any secrets, asking those present 'You know, don't you?'.

Sheila briefly tells Eric about Mrs Birling's attempts to blame the father of Eva's child, and we are reminded of Eric's drinking habit. Despite Sheila's repeated attempts to reveal the truth, Mrs Birling still attempts to defend her son, denying his drinking problem. Eric briefly turns against Sheila, calling her a 'sneak', but this does not last long. He is soon asking for a drink before he begins the account of his relationship with Eva Smith. His father tries to stop him from having a drink but again, showing he is in control, the inspector allows it. Eric subsequently feels calm enough to tell his story.

He explains how he met Eva in the Palace Theatre bar (the same place Gerald had met Eva the previous November). He was drunk or, as he describes it, 'squiffy'. He bought drinks for Eva, accompanied her home and, despite her telling him that she did not want him to enter her lodgings, he insisted. He says he was 'in that state when a chap easily turns nasty'. It is implied that he forced his way in and had sex with Eva, 'And that's when it happened. And I don't even remember—that's the hellish thing'. At this point, Mr Birling insists that his shocked wife and daughter leave the room. This is a reminder that, at the time, many women were regarded as fragile and in need of protection from emotional as well as physical harm. Obviously, the Birlings had been less keen to protect the lower-class Eva in the same way.

Eric met Eva again a fortnight later. They slept together again and continued to have a sexual relationship until Eva informed Eric that she was pregnant with his child. Again, her sense of morality is highlighted when Eric explains that Eva did not want to marry him because she knew he did not love her. She demonstrated maturity, recognising that Eric could not give her stability. He complains that she treated him like a child.

At no stage does Eric mention Eva's name, so the confusion about her identity and whether the Birlings all met the same girl continues.

Eric gave Eva a sum of money, which he stole from his father's office. His parents are both shocked at this revelation; clearly they do not know their son nearly as well as they thought they did. Mr Birling immediately worries about covering up the crime, no doubt thinking about the need to uphold his reputation. Priestley is making the point that just because someone has money or has had a privileged upbringing, this does not mean they are destined to become moral pillars of society. Eric's relationship with his father has not helped the situation, with Eric feeling Mr Birling is 'not the kind of father a chap could go to when he's in trouble'.

Eva stopped accepting money from Eric when she realised it had been stolen. Again, she demonstrates that she is willing to do the right thing even if it means she is worse off. Eric is unaware until this moment that Eva had then visited Mrs Birling's charity committee to ask for help before being rejected. Eric laments that his mother is to blame for the deaths of the girl and his child because she was the final person Eva met (chronologically) in the 'chain of events' that resulted in her death: 'you turned her away—yes, and you killed her.'

This accusation sparks off a row between the family members, but the inspector soon intervenes and makes it clear that they all had a part to play in the death of Eva Smith. Goole reminds each of them of their roles; effectively, this serves as a reminder to the audience that the 'chain of events' is complete.

Next comes the inspector's powerful final speech. Inspector Goole's parting words are very important as they sum up the main message of the play. There are three key sections to consider. Firstly, 'One Eva Smith has gone—but there are millions and millions and millions of Eva Smiths and John Smiths still left with us'. Here, Priestley highlights that Eva Smith is actually a symbol, a representative of all other poor citizens in the community. The story has not finished with her death, as there are other women and men (John Smiths) who need looking after. It is essential that we all take responsibility for our actions towards others, including those less fortunate than ourselves.

This section is followed by possibly the most important lines in the entire play: 'We are members of one body. We are responsible for each other'. These words sum up Priestley's message of social responsibility. He threatens that if we do not learn this lesson, we will be taught it in 'fire and blood and anguish'. The audience will understand that he is predicting the horrors of two world wars. His predictions, unlike those of Mr Birling, and correct. The audience is therefore cleverly led to believe that Priestley's socialist views are also correct.

After this, the inspector departs, leaving the Birlings to talk over the events of the evening. The way the family talk to one another at this point in the play is in stark contrast to the way they spoke at the start of the play when they were celebrating Sheila's engagement to Gerald, unaware of how badly they had all behaved towards Eva Smith.

Sheila is the first to wonder whether or not Inspector Goole is actually a real inspector. Mr Birling chiefly blames Eric for what happened, but also insists that is certainly does matter if the inspector is real. Sheila recognises that it does not change their previous behaviour: they all still treated a young woman in the way they did.

Mrs Birling agrees with her husband that who Inspector Goole was makes a difference. Eric sides with Sheila, highlighting the difference between the generations and how the younger characters are willing to accept responsibility for their actions, unlike the older characters.

Upon Gerald's return, both Mr and Mrs Birling try to stop Sheila from telling him what has taken place since his departure, but it is clear that Gerald is preoccupied with something else, so the tension rises again. He explains how he met another police officer whilst he was out. This officer told him there was nobody on the force with the name Inspector Goole. Mr Birling is excited by this, believing that they no longer need to accept any responsibility; they have not been caught by anyone, so should not feel guilty. He rings the Chief Constable, who confirms what Gerald has said. There is no Inspector Goole on their staff.

Sheila and Eric remain upset whereas Mr and Mrs Birling relax, believing themselves to be the victims of a hoax. Eric understands that it does not matter whether the inspector is real.

It is Gerald who questions whether each of them has actually met the same woman. They all admitted what they had done but, Gerald explains, they did not all see the same photograph at the same time. More questions are raised about whether this matters. What if it was a different person? Does that excuse their actions? For example, does Sheila having an innocent woman sacked from Milwards not matter if that woman had not already been fired from another company some time before?

Mr Birling and Gerald suggest that no-one has died at all. Gerald rings the infirmary and learns that no-one has been brought in after drinking disinfectant; the infirmary has not seen a case of suicide for months. At this, Mr and Mrs Birling return to the mood of celebration that started the play. Sheila and Eric remain aware that each of them has treated a young woman badly, even if it might not have been the same person and even if nobody had committed suicide. Sheila and Eric have learnt to take responsibility for their actions towards others. Priestley's message of social responsibility has been learned by two of the younger 'more impressionable' generation.

Gerald tries to return to the situation that started the play by offering Sheila the engagement ring. She shows her independence and growth as a character by refusing, saying 'it's too soon'.

Just as Act 1 was interrupted by the 'sharp ring' of the doorbell, signalling the arrival of the inspector, it is at this point that the telephone 'rings sharply', interrupting their conversation. Mr Birling answers the phone and reveals that it is the police on the line: a young woman has died after swallowing disinfectant. An inspector is on his way to question them.

Quick Quiz: Act 3

1. Who is the final character to be questioned by the inspector?

2. What does Eric call his sister, Sheila, when she talks of his drinking habit?

3. Where did Eric meet Eva?

4. Eva had a relationship with Eric and became pregnant by him, but why did she not want to marry him?

5. How much money did Eric give Eva? Where did it come from?

6. How does Eric describe the relationship with his father?

7. Who does Eric blame for Eva's death?

8. Which two characters appear particularly distressed by their involvement in the 'chain of events'?

9. Who rings the Chief Constable to confirm Gerald's suspicions that Inspector Goole is not a real inspector?

10. What information is contained in the final phone call at the very end of the play?

Answers

1. Eric Birling.
2. A 'sneak'.
3. In the Palace Theatre bar – the same place as Gerald.
4. She knew he did not love her.
5. About 50 pounds, from his father's office.
6. He says Mr Birling was 'not a kind of father a chap could go to when he's in trouble'.
7. His mother, Mrs Birling. He says 'you turned her away – yes, and you killed her'.
8. Eric and Sheila.
9. Mr Birling.
10. That a young woman ('girl') has died after swallowing disinfectant, and an inspector is on his way to question the Birlings.

Form

In essays, some students make the mistake of calling 'An Inspector Calls' a novel and they write about reader response. Don't let this be you!

First and foremost, 'An Inspector Calls' is a **play**. The people on stage are **characters**, and those watching the play are the **audience**.

As you are aware, a play contains acts, which are sometimes subdivided into scenes. 'An Inspector Calls' is a three-act play.

A play is different to a novel or a poem in a number of important ways. For example, reading a novel is a solitary endeavor: you read it on your own, at your own pace. A play is experienced in a collective manner, with an audience experiencing together the action as it unfolds onstage. As Manfred Pfister points out in his fantastic book 'The Theory and Analysis of Drama':

'One consequence of the collective reception of dramatic texts is that the individual receiver is unable to vary the tempo of the reception process, nor can he usually interrupt it at will or have sections repeated if he has failed to understand the text. The reader of a novel, on the other hand, can determine his own reading speed, abandon or take up the text when he wishes, or even simply leaf through it forwards or backwards as his whim takes him.'

Here, then, is our first significant point to be aware of with 'An Inspector Calls' and indeed all works of drama: the audience is not in control. If they mishear a line of dialogue, they cannot revisit it. If they wish to refer back to an earlier event to check something, they cannot do so. If they are struggling to concentrate, they cannot put the text down and have a rest: they are a captive audience. Whilst the characters on-stage do all at least once escape the intensity of the action (not one character in 'An Inspector Calls' remains onstage throughout the play), the audience cannot. We, as the audience, are not granted even a moment's respite from the interrogation and its effects. Why is that? Perhaps because Priestley wants to challenge the audience with the message of the play, refusing to let up or give them respite from the intensity. This, then, means that drama is the perfect form for 'An Inspector Calls'. As Maggie B. Gale puts it in her book 'J.B. Priestley', 'Priestley maintained that theatre had the power to educate and to integrate and enliven a community, to help it think through the social issues which affected it.' Yes, it was in the setting of the theatre that Priestley truly felt he could challenge his audience.

With JB Priestley perhaps more than many other writers, the form of the text is of greater significance. Why? Because Priestley himself wrote successfully in many different forms. For example, he published over 25 novels: in fact he published more novels than plays. With this in mind we have to consider: why did Priestley choose to write 'An Inspector Calls' as a play? Would it have worked as well as a novel? Fortunately, we have the words of Priestley himself to answer these questions.

In 1947, shortly after writing 'An Inspector Calls', Priestley published a non-fiction work titled 'Theatre Outlook'. In this book he explains that he 'did not go to work in the Theatre and then discover, because it helped me to earn a living, that the Theatre is important. I left other kinds of writing, which offered me a safe living and far more piece of mind, to work in the Theatre because I believed the Theatre to be important.' The obvious question that springs to mind here is 'how and why is the Theatre important?'

Priestley goes on the explain that we must look at a play differently to other forms of literature. If we analyse simply the writer's use of language, for example, we offer no appreciation of the unique aspects of drama. We could, as he puts it 'enjoy all these, taking your own time, at home'. No, to Priestley there was something unique about theatre, and it is essential in 'An Inspector Calls'. He explains how, 'a genuine theatrical audience is not simply an assembly of individuals, all reacting as they would in private. Everything is heightened and felt more because in such an audience there is a collective response.'

He continues, 'you on your side cannot fully enjoy what is happening unless you lose your sense of separation from the people all round you, become part of the audience and indeed part of the whole performance, sharing the collective response and experience.'

So there it is: to Priestley, the form of drama refuses to allow the audience to experience the text in isolation and joins them together collectively. It is a form of literature which breaks down barriers and individualism, and forces a collective response. This of course ties in nicely with the main theme of the text: collective responsibility. The inspector's words, 'We are members of one body' adequately describe the collective nature of a theatre audience. Therefore we can argue that the form of the text actually helps to create a glimpse of the collective society Priestley is calling for.

Stage directions are extremely useful for analysing the playwright's intentions. For example, the detailed stage directions at the start of the play are for the director. The information about intended staging, props and lighting introduce the key themes of the play.

Other stage directions instruct actors how to perform. In a novel, the narrator explains a character's thoughts and feelings. In a play, we must rely on dialogue and stage directions to gain our insights and form our conclusions. How actors deliver lines can reveal a lot about the respective character. For example, after Mr Birling tells Mrs Birling to compliment the cook, Gerald agrees 'politely'. Like Mrs Birling, Gerald is aware that Mr Birling should not compliment a lower-class servant who is only doing her job. The stage direction 'politely' shows Gerald's good manners. As an upper-class gentleman, he is well bred, which is why he diplomatically agrees with his future father-in-law.

The play 'An Inspector Calls' contains a mixture of three genres. A genre is a category of literature that shares common literary techniques. These might be similarities in tone, plot, themes, settings and characters.

1. The Well Made Play
'An Inspector Calls' contains elements of a well made play, a concept coined by Eugene Scribe in the 19th century. Features of a well made play include:

Plot
There is one main story, and most of it happens before the play begins. In 'An Inspector Calls', the characters' interactions with Eva took place before the play begins.

Action and suspense increase through various devices, which might include:

> **Entrances and exits:** The timings of these must develop tension and increase suspense. For example, when Sheila sees the photograph of Eva, she leaves the stage in distress. Priestley increases tension by making the audience wait for her next entrance and her revelations.

> **Revelations about identity:** In the play, the 'chain of events' reveals that each character has influenced the life of Eva Smith who, it later transpires, is also Daisy Renton. Did they all meet the same young woman, however? The characters discuss this in Act 3, and Sheila and Eric link this to Priestley's message of social responsibility.

Complications: we see clashes between the inspector and the characters, clashes between the older and younger generations, and clashes in attitudes to class. These and other clashes have an important purpose: Priestley uses them to focus the attention of the audience on his socialist message, centred around the plot device of Eva Smith.

Exposition
At the beginning of the play, we are introduced to characters and relationships.

Climactic Curtain
This is where an act or scene ends on an incredibly tense and dramatic moment. For example, at the end of Act 1, when Sheila has confronted Gerald about his affair with Eva, the inspector enters and asks 'Well?'. Then the curtain falls, leaving the audience in suspense—they question how he knows about Gerald's affair with Eva.

Obligatory Scene
This is a scene essential to the play—a secret is revealed, which adds drama and tension. Although the acts are not subdivided into scenes, Inspector Goole's description of Eva's suicide with the disinfectant that 'burnt her inside out' could be interpreted as an obligatory scene. Because of this revelation, the inspector calls on the Birling household.

Dénouement
This scene at the end of the play ties up loose ends. We do not have this with 'An Inspector Calls'.

2. Detective Story or Whodunnit
The play can be liked to a Whodunnit murder mystery. A traditional Whodunnit contains a detective who questions suspects, analyses the facts, and narrows down from a list of numerous suspects to just one, revealing the criminal. At the same time, the audience enjoys piecing together the 'chain of events' and trying to work out who the culprit is.

'An Inspector Calls' begins with the death of Eva Smith, and the inspector forces the Birlings and Gerald to look back over the events to piece together who is responsible. Priestley inverts (turns upside down) this genre when Inspector Goole reveals that everyone is responsible for the death of Eva Smith. By inverting the audience's expectations of the genre, Priestley presents his key message of social responsibility, and he encourages the audience to consider their own actions to others. This is discussed in more detail in the character analysis of inspector Goole.

3. Morality Play
Popular in the Middle Ages, morality plays aimed to teach people lessons about how to behave. Actors played personifications of the Seven Deadly Sins, amongst other characters. The Seven Deadly Sins are pride, envy (jealousy), wrath (anger), sloth (laziness), avarice (greed), gluttony, lust.

The BBC Bitesize website points out that 'Mr Birling is greedy because he wants more money, Sheila is guilty of wrath and envy when she spitefully complains about Eva Smith and so on'. Let's now explore that idea in more detail.

In 'An Inspector Calls', the inspector encourages the characters to confess their sins and to repent. As with a morality play, the audience is expected to learn a moral message from this. Certainly, the inspector is full of moralistic sayings; for example, 'We are members of one body. We are responsible for each other'. The characters of the play might represent particular Deadly Sins:

Character	Deadly Sin	Comments
Mr Birling	Avarice/ Greed Gluttony	• Money: he is a capitalist, greedy for money and wanting more by exploiting others for 'lower costs and higher prices'. • Food and drink: elements of gluttony are on the table in the opening stage directions.
Mrs Birling	Pride Wrath	• Her husband's 'social superior', she is proud of her status and instructs others on how to behave. • She is 'prejudiced' against Sheila because of her class, and she also feels contempt towards working-class women ('girls of that class'). • She is angry with Eva when she learns that Eva has assumed the name of Mrs Birling.
Eric Birling	Lust Gluttony	• He feels entitled to force his attentions on Eva. He is also aware that prostitutes haunt the Palace Theatre bar, suggesting that this is not his first visit. • His appetite for alcohol contributes towards his behaviour.
Sheila Birling	Envy Wrath	• She is jealous that the dress suited Eva better than her. • She was furious when she saw Eva smile at the other shop assistant.
Gerald Croft	Lust	• Like Eric, Gerald has a sexual affair with Eva. Both men objectify Sheila by describing her appearance. • Gerald turns his attentions to Sheila when he offers her the ring at the end of the play.

When analysing the characters by using the Seven Deadly Sins, consider the extent to which they learn a moral lesson and the impact this has on the audience. The idea of there being 'seven deadly sins' is not a Biblical idea. It was a medieval creation suggesting that certain sins lead to death and others did not. However, the Bible's teaching on sin is that 'all have sinned and fall short of the glory of God' (Romans 3:23) and no sin is greater than another. With this in mind, the seven deadly sin analysis, whilst interesting, cannot accurately be viewed as Biblical imagery like the 'fire and blood and anguish' quote which certainly is Biblical (and is explored in the character analysis of Inspector Goole). More accurately, we can explore the wide range of 'sins' demonstrated as evidence that the play is aiming to challenge as many members of the audience as possible. The insinuation is that each member of the audience will be challenged by at least one of the characters' actions which they can relate to. By judging the characters, Priestley hopes that audience members will also reflect on their own behaviour.

Structure

Time as a Structural Feature
a. Chronology
When studying the play, we should consider the ways in which Priestley uses time. The play begins with the Birlings celebrating the engagement of Sheila to Gerald. Here is a reminder of the events in chronological order that took place before the arrival of the inspector:

Date	'Chain of events'
September 1910	Mr Birling sacks Eva from Birling & Co.
December 1910	Eva begins work at Milwards.
Late January 1911	Sheila complains about Eva, who is then sacked.
March 1911	Eva changes her name to Daisy Renton and becomes Gerald's mistress.
September 1911	Gerald breaks off his affair with Eva. Eva leaves Brumley for two months.
November 1911	Eric meets Eva.
December 1911/January 1912	Eva finds out she is pregnant.
March 1912	Eva asks for help from the Brumley Women's Charity Organisation but is refused by Mrs Birling.
April 1912	Eva commits suicide.

The story of Eva Smith and each person's role in her life is revealed gradually by the inspector, providing time for the audience to consider each character's role in relation to Priestley's socialist message.

b. Dramatic Irony
The fact that the play is set in 1912 but first performed in 1945 enables Priestley to use dramatic irony. Dramatic irony is a technique used which allows the audience to know something which a character does not. Priestley uses this when Mr Birling makes statements about the Titanic being 'unsinkable' and when he says the 'Germans don't want war'. Any audience, whether in 1945 when the play was first performed, or today, would know that not only did the Germans play a key part in World War II, but the Titanic also sank. Priestley's effective use of dramatic irony instantly devalues Birling's opinions.

This means that when Birling follows his predictions with statements like 'community and all that nonsense', the audience is encouraged by Priestley to believe that Birling is continuing to talk rubbish. Priestley effectively gets the audience to agree with his own socialist views that community is, in fact, far from 'nonsense'.

Nearer the end of the play, the audience and Sheila have worked out that Eric is the father of Eva's child, but Mrs Birling is unaware of this when she says 'Go and look for the father of the child. It's his responsibility'. Priestley's use of dramatic irony helps to build tension and excitement, encouraging the audience to pay more attention to Priestley's message of social responsibility.

c. Foreshadowing

This device is an advance warning of what will happen later in the play. For example, at the start of the play, Sheila voices suspicions about Gerald's behaviour last summer when he was often absent. This comment builds tension and foreshadows the conflict to come when we later learn that Gerald was having an affair with Eva Smith.

d. The Future

Priestley does not dwell solely on the events of the past. The whole point of the play is to show that people can make a positive contribution to society if they accept responsibility for their actions and learn from their mistakes. It is about learning from the past to improve the future.

Interestingly, Priestley studied the concept of time, so it is not surprising that he experiments with it in the play. He considered Ouspensky's theory which suggests that, when we die, we re-start our lives if we have failed to learn from our mistakes.

Priestley also studied Dunne's theory, which again focuses on learning from mistakes. This theory proposes that we have all been given the ability to look forward in time so that we can avoid errors before we make them (as well as learn from mistakes in our past).

The idea of learning from mistakes is certainly a key idea in 'An Inspector Calls'. It is as if Inspector Goole is able to look into the future and know that another inspector is on his way. He encourages the characters to reflect on their behaviour towards Eva, and he gives them the opportunity to learn from their mistakes.

With the final telephone call at the end of the play, the Birlings and Gerald learn that a young lady has died from drinking disinfectant. There is also the puzzling news that an inspector is on his way to the Birling household to ask some questions. Perhaps Priestley is applying ideas from Ouspensky and Dunne to suggest that everything is going to happen again so that, this time, the reluctant characters of Mr Birling, Mrs Birling and Gerald Croft have the opportunity to learn the error of their ways.

By playing with time, Priestley might be suggesting that we cannot avoid taking responsibility for our actions.

Characters

Edna

In 'An Inspector Calls', every character is in some way representative of a section of society—through the character of Edna, Priestley demonstrates the mistreatment of the domestic working class.

Although Edna is a minor character in the play, there are a couple of key moments worthy of analysis. Firstly, it is Edna who shows Inspector Goole into the dining room in Act 1, announcing 'an inspector's called'. This line of dialogue is the closest line we have in the play to the title 'An Inspector Calls'. By putting the words in Edna's mouth, Priestley clearly establishes this as a significant moment. It symbolises that Priestley is giving a voice to the working classes, heralding new ways of thinking with his socialist ideas. Edna, a working-class woman, ushers in the inspector, who is about to challenge the values and beliefs held by the Birlings and Gerald.

Priestley also gives Edna the important task of changing the lighting in the room when the inspector arrives and Mr Birling commands 'Show him in here. Give us some more light'. The change of lighting on the stage moves from 'pink and intimate' to 'brighter and harder'. Here, Inspector Goole has a physical impact on the room, and the 'pink and intimate' lighting is indicative of the overly optimistic rose-tinted glasses through which the Birlings view their lives of middle-class privilege. Inspector Goole brings with him a harder sort of light—a spotlight of interrogation which will illuminate the truth. It is Edna who brings the inspector into the dining room and who changes the lighting: Priestley could be suggesting that it will be the working classes who will deliver the truth to the middle and upper classes. And this is what we see in the play—the life of working-class Eva Smith is used to challenge the Birlings and Gerald, making them face the true consequences of their actions. It is working-class Edna who brings in the inspector and changes the lighting that signifies that challenge.

We do not only analyse characters through how the speak and act, but also through how others speak to or about them. When Birling orders Edna to 'Show him in here. Give us some more light', the language and structure of his dialogue is worthy of analysis. As Tom Briars Delve points out, these two simple sentences are bluntly short and monosyllabic, suggesting no attempt at politeness from Birling to Edna. Both also start with clear imperatives, 'Show' and 'Give', as if Birling expects his orders to be followed instantly. Such off-hand comments may appear insignificant, but they subtly add to the dramatic force of Eva's narrative, highlighting the pressure on working-class women to unhesitatingly obey their middle-class employers, even if working conditions are unfair.

In 1912, when the play was set, the use of maids and servants in the homes of middle- and upper-class families was more common than by 1946 when the play was first performed in England. To the 1946 audience, Edna's very presence on stage would feel old-fashioned, and Priestley's deliberate inclusion of a maid would serve as a reminder to the audience of the outdated practice of employing working-class people for very little money to work long hours, completing jobs that could have easily been done by the owners of the house. For example, Edna is ordered to pour port, serve food, answer the door: none of the tasks she completes require any special skill, and they could all be done by the Birling family themselves. In fact, when Mr Birling offers to answer the door himself late into Act 3, Mrs Birling casually remarks 'Edna'll go. I asked her to wait up'. This intrusion into Edna's life demonstrates how the Birlings see Edna as merely an employee. They do not care that their actions are impinging upon her wellbeing. Edna cannot sleep because the Birlings want her up to do more tasks for them, even though we can assume that typically she would have finished work by this time.

It is also worth noting that the Birlings' successes are never shared with Edna; for example, she is not invited to join in the toast for the engagement. Priestley seems to be condemning this mistreatment of the working class—when the play was first performed in two theatres in Moscow in 1945, her character would have confirmed communist beliefs about the lazy, wealthy elite living a life of privilege at the expense of the poor. The 1946 London audience, however, would consider the treatment of Edna as out of date and overly formal. This would further alienate the Birlings from the audience, presenting them as people whose views and attitudes you would not wish to replicate or repeat.

Although Edna speaks only a few lines on stage, she still has more of a voice than Eva. Both Edna and Eva are two women from the working class, and both seem to suffer in some way at the hands of the Birlings. Eva never appears on stage, and yet her voice is channeled through Inspector Goole. When Goole tells the Birlings 'There are millions and millions and millions of Eva Smiths and John Smiths', he is advocating the absent Eva, who is unable to speak up for herself; however, there is also no one who speaks up for Edna. Edna's silence could be interpreted as symbolic of the lack of power that the working poor had. Women were not given the vote until 1918, six years after the play is set, and only women over the age of 30 with minimum property qualifications could vote. This would have excluded working-class women like Edna, who had to wait until 1928 before they were given the vote. Edna's silence therefore represents how working-class women had no voice in society and could not vote, so had no political voice to influence how society was run.

Edna would not have had the same freedom of movement as those in the middle classes, but she would have been even more restricted due to living with the Birlings. Her situation would have been more awkward if she had ever wanted to leave and ask for references. In 1912, employees did not have the same working rights as they did in 1946. The later strengthening of the unions meant a contemporary audience would appreciate how precarious Edna's position would have been had she wished to leave.

To conclude, Priestley might not use Edna to say very much, but it is just as important to consider what is not said when viewing her importance in the play. The working poor suffered in many ways, and not all of them are obvious at first glance. Through his depiction of Edna, Priestley encourages us to consider how, even when they are being paid, the poor are exploited.

Eva Smith

How exactly do you analyse a character who never appears on-stage and has no dialogue in a play? Despite holding a central role in 'An Inspector Calls', the audience never meets Eva Smith. However, Priestley uses Eva's lack of voice and presence on stage to symbolise the lack of power held by women and the working class in Edwardian England.

Priestley's choice of names carries symbolic significance when it comes to the character of Eva Smith and her alias Daisy Renton. Firstly, the name 'Eva' can be seen as an intertextual Biblical reference to Eve the first woman, and the person from whom we are all descended. Combined with the common surname 'Smith', Priestley seems to be suggesting that in Eva Smith, we see a woman who symbolises all women. Inspector Goole suggests as much in his final speech when he explains 'there are millions and millions and millions of Eva Smiths'. The name choice makes it clear that Priestley does not want his audience to feel sorry for one working class woman. Instead, he wants us to consider Eva Smith as representing all working-class women. Her name is used to provide an important lesson on how to treat those who suffer the effects of inequality in society.

The second name Eva Smith adopts is Daisy Renton, and this name is also interesting in terms of Priestley's use of symbolism. A daisy is a common flower, cheap and pretty, and in this way could be seen as symbolic of Eva Smith: she is repeatedly described as pretty, but is obviously one of many working-class women. As we have already explored, it is quite shocking just how often Eva Smith is described in terms of her physical appearance. Therefore, the name Daisy, with its connotations of prettiness, seems quite appropriate as a symbol of how this young woman was judged largely on her physical appearance.

The surname 'Renton' could have different interpretations. On the one hand, the verb 'rent' means to pay for using something for a period of time; as Daisy Renton, Eva rents her body when she enters a life of prostitution. Alternatively, the noun 'rent' is also a large tear in a piece of fabric. This might symbolise that, at this point in Eva's life, her spirit has been broken. She has left respectable society, and is now trying to exist in the underworld of crime. In both name choices, Priestley therefore uses symbolism.

Priestley uses descriptions of her appearance by others to show how women were objectified in Edwardian England. Firstly, Mr Birling describes Eva Smith as a 'lively good-looking girl'. Sheila states that Eva was 'a very pretty girl too—with big dark eyes'. Gerald's words echo those of Sheila, as he describes Eva as being 'very pretty—soft brown hair and big dark eyes'. Even Inspector Goole says 'she had been pretty—very pretty'. These descriptions all focus on Eva's physical appearance and beauty, and they highlight the way in which women were objectified. They were regarded as sources of pleasure for men, rather than as equals.

The character of Eva is also used to draw the attention of the audience to a clear double standard for men and women at the time. It is worth, at this point, pausing to think about the 'trouble' Eva Smith was in. She was pregnant outside of marriage and had no means of providing for herself financially. Eva lied to the charity committee, saying she was married, because admitting to having had sex outside of marriage would have made her unlikely to receive help from the charity. However, the same high moral standards were not expected of men. At the start of Act 3, when it is revealed that Eric slept with Eva, impregnated her and stole money from his father's business, it is the stolen money that features most heavily in the parental reprimand from Mr Birling. In fact, Eric excuses the sexual relationship by telling his father 'Well, I'm old enough to be married, aren't I?'. Birling himself earlier admits that he and his peers in their younger years also 'broke out and had a bit of fun sometimes'. Gerald, too, excuses his affair, explaining that 'I suppose it was inevitable. She was young and pretty'. As so often happens in this play, the inspector sums it up perfectly when he explains how Eric treated Eva 'as if she was an animal, a thing, not a person'. This quotation summarises nicely the way in which women were objectified by men as sources of pleasure, not equals.

Eva, on the other hand, is a hard worker, and has strong moral values which see her refuse to accept stolen money. Yet Eva is the one who feels forced to commit suicide whereas the men of the play seem to have (up until now) suffered no ill consequences for their actions. These double standards can be seen as relating to gender or class, and the message is clear: women/the working class cannot get away with the poor behaviour and actions that men/ the middle and upper class can.

As the play progresses, Priestley presents Eva as a character who has suffered from the imbalance of power. Mr Birling's power as employer led to her losing her first job at the factory. Sheila's power as a prized customer led to her losing her second job at Milwards. Eric's physical power allowed him to gain entry into Eva's lodgings, and Gerald's upper-class power enabled him to control her. Gerald was only able to provide Eva with somewhere to stay and give her money because of his upper-class privilege and connections. The result of this is that Eva became totally reliant on him: as Sheila observed, Gerald was Eva's 'fairy prince'. It's worth noting how the relationship between Eva and Gerald contrasts with that of Gerald and Sheila. With Gerald and Sheila, the audience have seen from Act 1 a playfulness between the two, with Sheila willing to tease Gerald and tell him that she does not wish him to become a 'purple-faced' expert in port. The contrast between the two women, and Gerald's treatment of them, is interesting because Sheila observes that Gerald would have 'adored it', implying that there is something about Gerald's character that craves a partner who is subservient, and perhaps feeds his ego. Eva Smith's compliance and naivety, even down to Gerald's patronising comment on her port and lemonade drink as 'some such concoction' reveals his sneering attitude towards the working class, and his pleasure over the power he had over her.

Finally, Priestley uses the character of Eva to convey his message about social responsibility when, in the inspector's exit speech, he states 'One Eva Smith has gone—but there are millions and millions and millions of Eva Smiths and John Smiths still left with us'. Priestley's use of repetition and the rule of three with the word 'millions' develops rhythm and momentum, building up to his point about the quantity of vulnerable poor still living. It is at this point that the inspector states that it is not just women who are vulnerable but also working-class men (the name John is a very common name, like the surname Smith). Women, however, are more open to exploitation by men like Eric and Gerald. Priestley now positions the inspector to be the champion of all the poor, regardless of gender.

Mr Birling

Mr Birling represents all the negative aspects of capitalism. As a member of the older generation, he is fixed in his ways—we see no change in his character throughout the play, and he remains unsympathetic to the plight of Eva Smith.

In his 1957 nonfiction book 'Theatre Outlook', JB Priestley states that everything on stage in a play is significant. With this in mind, we will analyse Mr Birling in relation to a prop in the opening line of the play. In the play's first line of dialogue, Mr Birling says: 'Giving us the port, Edna? That's right. You ought to like this port, Gerald. As a matter of fact, Finchley told me it's exactly the same port your father gets from him'. The drinking of port is significant due to its cost. It is something that was associated with the wealthy in society: the price alone would have been prohibitive and therefore out of reach for the working class. We should also remember that the characters have been drinking another expensive drink, evidenced by the 'champagne glasses', before the play begins.

In her fascinating book 'Drinking in Victorian and Edwardian Britain, Beyond the Spectre of the Drunkard', Thora Hands states: 'The domestic context of alcohol consumption was governed by rules of social etiquette, which both demonstrated and reinforced social class and gender values. Within middle- and upper-class homes, purchasing, serving and consuming good quality wines and spirits were key ways to demonstrate levels of cultural capital and good taste'. Instantly, the audience sees Mr Birling as someone who wishes to show off to others, and Priestley uses the name dropping of 'Finchley' to illustrate how Birling is keen to impress his future son-in-law. It is important to note that, in speaking to Gerald, the son of upper-class Lord and Lady Croft, Birling is actually speaking to his social superior. This imbalance of power has reduced him to name-dropping in an attempt to endear himself to a family whose social position is one to which he personally aspires. Birling himself has moved from working class to middle class through the success of his business, which is why he occasionally has to be told how to behave socially by Mrs Birling, described in the stage directions as his 'social superior'.

Early in Act 1, Priestley surprises the audience when Birling delivers a speech to his family during the engagement meal that does not—as the audience might expect—focus on his love for his daughter or his fondness of his future son-in-law. Instead, his speech centres on his opinions of the economic future of the country and the failings of neighbouring nations. This speech is an excellent example of Priestley presenting Mr Birling as a flawed, misled and pompous man. He refers to himself twice in very similar ways, first as a 'hard-headed business man' and then moments later as a 'hard-headed, practical man of business'. This deliberate repetition on Priestley's part emphasises how Mr Birling's self-perception is entirely built upon how he sees himself in terms of work and money. Mr Birling's priorities are not with people or family, but with how much wealth he can accumulate. As he himself puts it, 'a man has to mind his own business and look after himself and his own'. It is significant that he places himself first, and his family come second, almost as an afterthought. By ordering Mr Birling's priorities in this way, Priestley depicts Birling as a selfish man, who prioritises making money and looking after himself over his family. It is therefore unsurprising when we learn of his lack of empathy towards Eva Smith and his exploitative capitalist outlook.

Mr Birling can be seen to represent the ideology of capitalism—a system where business is privately owned for the sole purpose of making profit. Of course, to make this profit, business owners must 'keep labour costs down' as Birling explains. As we later learn, Birling's capitalist agenda is one of the causes of Eva Smith's death. Birling's viewpoint will be directly contrasted by the message soon to be delivered by Inspector Goole, whom Birling will later dismiss as 'Probably a Socialist'.

Priestley uses an almost ridiculous amount of dramatic irony (where the audience knows something that the character on stage does not) to ridicule the character of Mr Birling. Given that the play was set in 1912 but first performed in 1945 in Moscow and 1946 in England, contemporary audiences knew that Mr Birling's predictions are wrong. His confidence that 'The Germans don't want war', for example, is doubly wrong, given that not one, but two world wars would in fact take place in the coming years. Like many others in the early 1900s, Mr Birling claims the idea of war is 'nonsense' and 'fiddlesticks'. His dismissive tone reveals how confident he is in his ideas. His error filled predictions about war, economic growth, and the Titanic being 'absolutely unsinkable' make him seem ill informed and ridiculous. This in turn encourages the audience to mistrust his capitalist views about business and the treatment of his own employees. Priestley's effective use of dramatic irony means Mr Birling's opinions are instantly devalued. Structurally, these examples of dramatic irony occur so early on in the play—even before the arrival of the inspector—to make it very clear that Mr Birling and everything he stands for is wrong.

Initial impressions of Mr Birling are not good, but that can be also said of other characters (for example, see our analysis of Sheila). However, what is so noticeable about Mr Birling is how he ends the play in the same manner in which he started. For example, near the end of the play, Birling discovers that his son, Eric, is an alcoholic who has stolen money from the office and impregnated Eva Smith. It might therefore be surprising to the audience that the majority of his dialogue with Eric focuses solely on recovering his lost money. Eric's slight against him and the impact upon his business cause Mr Birling consternation—not the death of his grandchild or the alcoholism of his son.

Priestley employs contrast between the older and younger generations to make a point about capitalism and socialism. Unlike his children, Mr Birling fails to accept responsibility for the death of Eva Smith, telling Eric 'There's every excuse for what both your mother and I did'. Birling fails to learn the inspector's (and Priestley's) lesson of social responsibility, reinforcing the inspector's earlier comments about how it is the 'young ones' who are 'more impressionable'. Priestley is criticising the behaviour of the older generation, implying that they are fixed in their ways. In contrast, the younger generation of the Birling family is open to new socialist ideas.

Mrs Birling

JB Priestley uses the character of Mrs Birling to criticise the inequalities of the class system and to highlight the gender bias evident within Edwardian society. The topic of social class was an incredibly important theme to Priestley. As Maggie B Gale puts it in her book 'J.B. Priestley', 'Priestley's belief that the class system and easy manner in which power had essentially remained in the hands of the few - despite the genuine upheaval of war - underpinned much of his writing and especially his plays'. Priestley was frustrated with the ingrained class system, and he uses Mrs Birling to criticise this system.

One of the ways he achieves this is through his negative depiction of Mrs Birling as bossy and controlling. We read in the opening stage directions that Mrs Birling is 'her husband's social superior', and this is certainly the role she exhibits within her family. Much of the initial dialogue afforded to her character is based on controlling and reprimanding the actions of others. Here are a few examples, taken from just the opening five pages of Act 1:

'(Reproachfully) Arthur, you're not supposed to say such things—'

'Now, Sheila, don't tease him.'

(To Sheila and Eric) 'Now stop it, you two.'

'Arthur, what about this famous toast of yours?'

(To Arthur) 'I don't think you ought to talk business on an occasion like this.'

'I think Sheila and I had better go into the drawing-room and leave you men.'

(To Arthur) 'don't keep Gerald in here too long.'

'Eric—I want you a minute.'

By establishing Mrs Birling as a controlling and demanding character, Priestley positions her as a self-important woman who is used to giving orders and being obeyed. Much of her dialogue reveals a concern for actions that might give a bad impression (presumably to Gerald who is, at this point, the only character on stage from outside the family). Although Mrs Birling is her husband's 'social superior', she is still of a lower status than Gerald. Her ease with giving orders and her expectation of being obeyed might also foreshadow how she uses her position on the committee of the Brumley Women's Charity Organization to influence its members to deny help to Eva Smith/Daisy Renton.

Priestley establishes Mrs Birling as bossy and controlling at the start of the play in order to set up the inevitable conflict with Inspector Goole when he arrives. In Act 2, Mrs Birling complains that Inspector Goole's comments are 'a trifle impertinent' and in Act 3 describes his questioning as 'peculiar and offensive'. She is clearly used to having her own way and cannot understand why she cannot order the police inspector around. Priestley uses Mrs Birling's discomfort with a police inspector refusing to obey her as an example of the wealthy middle and upper classes' complacency when it comes to the law. Both Birling and Mrs Birling namedrop people they know in the police, expecting Inspector Goole to give them an easier time. When people use their connections to avoid prosecution, we call this corruption. Mr and Mrs Birling clearly see themselves as above the law, and they struggle when faced with someone who is moral and insisting that justice is served.

Priestley uses Mrs Birling as a dramatic device to develop tension. Of all the characters, it is Mrs Birling who is the most resistant to confess her connection to Eva Smith. Mr Birling and Sheila explain their link as soon as they realise they know her; Gerald attempts to lie to Inspector Goole, but almost immediately thinks better of it and confesses. Mrs Birling, however, lies outright for two pages ('No. Why should I?') before finally admitting that she recognises Eva. However, even once Inspector Goole has prized this admission out of her, she defends herself and dodges questions until the very end of Act 2. With every refusal to answer, Priestley raises tension—he makes the audience wait for her confession. This is heightened by his superb use of dramatic irony when the audience works out that Eric is the father of Eva Smith's child, but Mrs Birling is completely oblivious.

Mrs Birling seems to embody everything that Priestley disliked about the behaviour of the middle- and upper-class women of Edwardian society. In Priestley's radio show, he spoke about women who after the war were more concerned about their own lives than helping others. He described how he received bitter letters 'from ladies doing nothing in inland resorts, where their energy is all turned inward instead of outward, turning into hostility instead of helpfulness and fun'. Mrs Birling shares many characteristics with these women, and Priestley uses her as an example of how petty and self-centred (or egocentric) some people can be when they themselves live easy and comfortable lives, and others are struggling to eat.

The situation for women like Eva Smith was made worse by the lack of support from the government. In 1912, there was no NHS, no benefit system, and no access to contraception or abortions. Therefore, women were reliant upon charities to help them cope when they were struggling. Priestley uses the charity committee who are swayed by Mrs Birling's 'prejudiced' views to demonstrate how fallible this system was. It is also worth thinking about why someone like Mrs Birling helped out on a charity committee. Mrs Birling makes her opinions of the working classes clear: they are liars, they accept stolen money, and they are to blame for their own situations. If Mrs Birling has such a low opinion of the people she is meant to be helping, should she actually be helping them? We can infer that her ulterior motive to work on the committee has more to do with how it looks to chair such a committee and to wield power. She certainly does not strike the audience as a person driven by the desire to help other people.

Priestley employs the prop of bells to present another sign of Mrs Birling's privilege. Mrs Birling tells Edna she will 'ring' from the drawing room when she needs her—this system of bells for maids later fell out of common usage by 1946. Priestley famously claimed in 1927 that the practice of having domestic servants, was 'as obsolete as the horse'. The Birling family's use of domestic staff highlights the 'old' ways of doing things where working-class women were made to work in difficult conditions for very little money. The increase of opportunities to work in other industries, the outbreak of war, and the increased use of technology meant that housework was easier to perform. This meant that by 1946, domestic staff had greatly diminished in middle-class homes. Priestley's inclusion of Edna and Mrs Birling's ordering her about emphasise how out of date the Birlings are in the eyes of his audience and, by default, how archaic their thinking about capitalism was. The notion of being privileged runs through the play: characters who are apparently unaware of their privilege take advantage of others who are less privileged than themselves. Priestley questions the morality of Edwardian society through his depiction of a privileged family and their attitudes towards others who are less fortunate than themselves.

Priestley uses the character of Mrs Birling to develop the theme of gender. (We see, for example, how Eva Smith is objectified by Gerald and Eric. We also see how Sheila is infantilised by her parents.) Even Mrs Birling suffers the inequality of gender treatment. Despite Mrs Birling's 'social' superiority, she still behaves in a subservient manner to her husband. Indeed, she promotes the idea of female submission to her own daughter, excusing Gerald's neglect of his relationship with Sheila, telling her 'When you're married, you'll realise that men with important work to do sometimes have to spend nearly all their time and energy on their business'. Mrs Birling accepts that women must come second to their husbands' work. We also see later in the play that Mrs Birling is unaware of the fact that Eric has a drink problem. Women are seen to be delicate and in need of protection from the real world, and it is not only men who force this expectation on women, but women who accept it.

Mrs Birling's attitude to alcohol is another way in which she conforms to stereotypical gender roles. In Edwardian England, middle- and upper-class women did not have the same freedom to drink as men. Thora Hands points out in her book 'Drinking in Victorian and Edwardian Britain, Beyond the Spectre of the Drunkard':

'Dinner parties were some of the few social occasions where middle-and upper-class women could drink for gratification and do so in a manner that was deemed respectable. The same degree of moral scrutiny and control did not apply to the drinking habits of middle- and upper-class men, for whom dinner parties in the home were only one potential site of alcohol consumption.'

Mrs Birling is reluctant to drink alcohol—when pushed by her husband, she agrees to drink 'Just a little'; this attitude to alcohol directly contrasts with that of her son, Eric, and potential future son-in-law, Gerald, who both go out drinking in Brumley. Priestley is not suggesting, of course, that women should get blind drunk like Eric: he is simply drawing attention to the double standard with which they are treated.

In conclusion, Priestley's message about gender is the same as his message about class: all inequality is morally wrong, and everyone, no matter what class or gender, should be treated with equality. Through Mrs Birling, Priestley gives a scathing critique of Edwardian England, a society where those with privilege are blind to the struggles of those without. He warns against the consequences of ignoring your privilege with the play's brutal ending, where the characters who have not learned their lessons will be punished for their arrogance.

Eric Birling

Priestley uses the character of Eric to represent young, impulsive, ignorant middle-class men, who exploit working-class women like Eva Smith for their own sexual gratification. By the end of the play, Eric has changed. He regrets what he has done and sympathises with the inspector's views on social responsibility. Priestley uses the change in Eric's character to show the audience that every young man can choose between exploiting the weak or adopting Priestley's ideas about social responsibility.

At the beginning of the play, Priestly uses stage directions to present Eric as not fully mature. He is 'half shy, half assertive'. The adjective 'shy' connotes nervousness and a lack of confidence. This contrasts with 'assertive', which implies confidence and dominance. Priestley's use of contrasting adjectives therefore creates a sense of confusion, implying that he is a secretive person. From the beginning of the play, it is clear that Priestley wants the audience to view Eric negatively in order to show that the capitalist patriarchal society is not trustworthy. This way, he encourages the audience to reject the capitalist ideas that Eric appears to be representing. There is hope, however: Priestley repeats the word 'half' to emphasise that Eric's character is not yet fully formed—this indicates that he might change.

From the start of the play, Priestley associates Eric with alcohol when his sister, Sheila, accuses him of being 'squiffy'. This contemporary slang, meaning slightly drunk, draws the attention of the audience to Sheila's use of informal language. It positions the Birling siblings as fashionable members of the younger generation who adapt their language to the times. This foreshadows both characters adapting their attitudes to social responsibility as the play unfolds and they become more sympathetic to the inspector's message.

In addition, Priestley deliberately aligns Eric with alcohol to foreshadow the later revelations about his drunken behaviour on the night that he met Eva Smith. Eric's free and easy use of alcohol is also used to signify the double standard in society for men and women (seethe character analysis of Mrs Birling, above).

When Eric is interrogated by the inspector, the audience learns that he insisted on entering Eva's lodgings. He admits that because of alcohol, he was 'in that state when a chap easily turns nasty'. Priestley's use of the determiner 'that' is interesting because Eric appears to be appealing to a commonly shared belief that his listeners have been drunk and understand exactly what 'that state' is. This shows his lack of responsibility for his actions and also suggests that he is using alcohol to excuse for his later implied rape of Eva. The playwright develops this idea when Eric refers to himself in the third person with the phrase 'a chap'. The word 'chap', an informal word for a boy or a man, has positive connotations of friendliness. Eric's use of the third person also distances him from the implied rape. By using these words, Eric is positioning himself as a friendly young man, who does not take responsibility for his behaviour, which is solely due to the alcohol.

Priestley presents us with Eric's perspective about Eva, so we do not know the exact details of whether she was a prostitute. If Eva was not working as a prostitute, she seemed to be living a life on the brink of prostitution. Prostitution, and the word prostitute would not be used in the play—at that time, other plays had been censored for making references to prostitutes. In fact, one of Priestley's playwright friends, George Bernard Shaw (whom he references when Mr Birling is naming people he does not agree with in Act 1) wrote a play called 'Mrs Warren's Profession', which was about a woman who was once a madam of a brothel. The play was banned by the theatre censors, and its actors were even arrested during one performance.

From the clues provided by Eric in his confession, Priestley provides an insight into a male perspective of sex workers. Eric is aware of the purpose of the Palace Theatre bar, and describes Eva as 'not the usual sort', saying that there 'was some woman who wanted her to go there'. This woman, we can presume, would have been Eva's madam, the woman who would have taken a cut of the money Eva would have made from performing sexual acts. We are told that Eric 'never quite understood about that'. Eric's ignorance could be construed as a wilful ignoring of the facts—a cognitive dissonance, detaching himself from his actions and his beliefs. We know from the beginning of the play that he has a sympathy for the working class—particularly when he argues with his father that the factory workers 'can't go and work somewhere else' if the pay does not suit them. Is it possible that Eric has developed this sympathy as a consequence of his relationship with a woman from the working class? Or because he is naturally sympathetic? Priestley is definitely hinting that Eric has the potential (even before his confession to Inspector Goole) to be sympathetic to the plight of the poor, which ties in with Inspector Goole's assertion that 'the young ones' are 'more impressionable'.

With Eric's next words, the audience understands that he now takes responsibility and he admits his guilt. Priestley uses short sentences and a hyphen to reveal Eric's distress: 'And that's when it happened. And I don't even remember—that's the hellish thing'. His lack of detail about what happened suggests that he can barely bring himself to admit what he has done. The sentence 'And that's when it happened', implying rape, allows us to form our own conclusions about what happened that night. This makes his behaviour more shocking. By describing this moment, Priestley heightens the contrast at the end of the play when we see exactly how much Eric's character has changed.

Priestley also presents Eric as an immature young man who does not have a close relationship with his father. He tells Mr Birling that he is 'not the kind of father a chap could go to when he's in trouble'. Again, by using the friendly word 'chap' to describe himself, he is making excuses for his behaviour by positioning himself as a victim rather than accepting responsibility for his behaviour. At this point in the play, we see Eric's immaturity because he is providing short-term solutions (by asking Eva to marry him and supporting her with stolen money), but he does not see the long-term consequences of his criminal behaviour.

By the end of the play, Eric, like Sheila, has learned the lesson of collective social responsibility. The discussion about whether the inspector is real does not matter to Eric, who insists 'We did her in all right'. He deliberately uses the plural personal pronoun 'we' to emphasise that it is not just his mother who is responsible for Eva's death, but all of them. This might symbolise Priestley's socialist view that we all have a collective responsibility for the welfare of Eva and other vulnerable members of society. Eric also states: 'It's what happened to the girl and what we all did to her that matters'. He has accepted his role in her downfall, and the inspector's socialist message of collective responsibility is more important than the identity of the inspector. Eric's language therefore echoes that of the inspector, the mouthpiece of Priestley.

Throughout the play, Priestley has presented Eric as an immature young man with a drinking problem, an exploiter of Eva, and a thief. As Eric matures and accepts responsibility for his actions, he becomes receptive to the inspector's message that 'We are members of one body. We are responsible for each other'. Because Eric, a member of the younger generation, changes, he represents hope that other young men in the audience will also take Priestley's message to heart. Eric, like Sheila, symbolises hope for the future.

Sheila Birling

Priestley presents Sheila as a spoilt, immature girl, who develops into an independent woman. As the play progresses, she aligns herself with the inspector and challenges her parents' capitalist views. Her character symbolises the growing independence of free-thinking young women, perhaps echoing the rise of the suffragette movement. By the end of the play, Sheila realises that she has more options than the traditional route of marriage. Through Sheila, Priestley shows us that socialism has the power to develop the spiritual and emotional growth of women.

In the opening moments of the play, Priestley presents Sheila as an immature, materialistic character. Despite the stage directions telling us that she is 'in her early twenties', Sheila refers to her parents as 'Mummy' and 'Daddy', an infantile, immature mode of address which is reciprocated by Mr and Mrs Birling, who refer to Sheila as both a 'child' and 'childish'. Sheila's comment about the engagement ring and how she will 'never let it go out of my sight' presents her as materialistic, as does the comment from Eric that Sheila and Mrs Birling are 'talking about clothes' when they retire to the drawing room in Act One.

We see numerous examples where Priestley presents other characters treating Sheila as inferior. Early in Act One, Gerald enquires of Sheila, 'I've been trying long enough, haven't I?', but it is Mrs Birling who interrupts and replies in Sheila's place, telling Gerald 'Of course she does'. Later, Gerald tries to have Sheila removed from the room during his interrogation, telling the inspector in the opening of Act Two, 'I think Miss Birling ought to be excused'. Yes, it is clear early on that Sheila is not treated as an equal by anyone. And why is that? In Edwardian England women were treated as inferior to men. I mean, just take a quick look at Eric—he is undoubtedly more immature than Sheila, but he isn't treated like a child in the way she is. Sheila's treatment by others reflects how women were considered as having an inferior role within a male-dominated society. This attitude to women as inferior is, it can be argued, one of the causes of Eva Smith's death. Like Eva, Sheila is treated as inferior because of her gender. However, because she is middle class, she is more protected and less vulnerable than Eva Smith.

After the inspector's interrogation, Sheila begins to change as a character. Her words to Gerald of 'you fool – he knows' demonstrate a dramatic shift in her personality: the little girl who was cooing over a ring has gone, and her passivity has been replaced with a fiery indignation. The sarcastic 'you're forgetting I'm supposed to be engaged to the hero' cuts through Gerald's attempt to romanticise the story of his interactions with Eva. Furthermore, the maturity behind her cool returning of the ring, as opposed to her tantrum at the end of Gerald's confession, implies to the audience that this is a woman who is now not governed by her emotions – but by logic and reason.

Priestley seems to be suggesting that the audience should aspire to be like Sheila: they should own the mistakes they've made and make others accountable for their own mistakes too.

Priestley presents Sheila as a character who quickly learns the inspector's message of social responsibility, unlike her parents who, when they think they've got away with it, laugh and encourage their children to do the same, complaining, 'they can't even take a joke'. The contrast between Sheila and her parents can been interpreted as Priestley criticising the behaviour of the older generation, who are fixed in their ways.

To signify this change in Sheila's character, we see a shift in the terms of address she uses with her parents. In Act Two, Sheila addresses Mrs Birling as 'Mother' and Mr Birling as 'Father'– a symbol of how she has matured from the childlike Act 1 address of 'Mummy' and 'Daddy'.

Also in Act Two, Sheila interrupts and answers a question directed at Mrs Birling, telling the inspector 'Yes, she is. Why?' when the inspector asks Mrs Birling if she is a member of the Brumley

Women's Charity Organization. This is a dramatic turnaround from the start of the play where it was Mrs Birling interrupting and answering for Sheila. The change in Sheila is dramatic and serves as an example to the audience of how they too can dramatically change for the better.

With the inspector's final exit in Act Three, Sheila can in some ways be seen to take on his role. We saw a hint of this at the end of Act One, when it was Sheila who forced a confession out of Gerald whilst the inspector went off stage with Eric. Following the inspector's departure in the third act, Sheila interrogates her family and Gerald, asking a series of questions. Through this use of questioning, Priestley is showing how Sheila has taken on the interrogating role of the inspector.

Priestley also uses repetition as a technique, with Sheila mirroring the language used previously by the inspector when she talks about 'Fire and blood and anguish' – the exact words previously spoken by the Inspector Goole. This mirroring of language is Priestley's way of showing us how Sheila has not only learned the Inspector's valuable lesson, but she has in some way taken on the role of the inspector himself. Yes, she realises her own fault in the matter, but she also wants to ensure that others do too.

Through his presentation of Sheila, Priestley encourages the audience to challenge conventional thinking and to question the behaviour of others – holding those to account who have power over us, even if that means rejecting those who are close to us and rethinking our own world views. If Sheila can so dramatically transform from a selfish, shallow character to one who now challenges others and cares about social responsibility, then everyone in the audience can also transform in the same way.

Gerald Croft

Gerald Croft is Priestley's tool to reveal the flaws of the upper classes. Priestley presents him as a stereotypical member of the upper classes. He represents the aristocracy who in 1912 exploited the working classes, especially working-class women like Eva Smith. For a moment in the play, he appears to be sorry for his behaviour towards Eva, providing hope that the upper classes can change and embrace Priestley's message of social responsibility. At the end of the play, however, he once again aligns himself with Mr Birling's capitalist ideas, conveying Priestley's view that the upper classes will always be self-interested and will never change.

When we first meet Gerald Croft, Priestley describes him in the introductory stage direction as an 'easy well-bred young man-about-town'. Priestley's use of the rule of three with the adjectives 'easy well-bred young' establish him as a member of a privileged, elite class, used to a life of leisure. It is surprising that the word 'young' is used when he had been described as roughly thirty years old. Perhaps Priestley is suggesting that his attitude towards life is immature and thoughtless; this foreshadows what we later learn about his irresponsible behaviour towards Eva and Sheila. It also raises false hope that, like the younger Birlings, Gerald will learn from his mistakes. The phrase 'man-about-town' shows that he is a fashionable socialite and implies experience in the ways of the world. It also implies vanity in that he prioritises himself (his appearance and his sexual needs) over helping others. This could foreshadow the later revelation that he used Eva Smith to satisfy his needs before discarding her when their relationship was no longer convenient. Bearing in mind the play was first performed in Moscow in 1945, Gerald's privileged appearance and demeanour would have confirmed communist beliefs about the lazy, wealthy elite living a life of privilege at the expense of the poor. The 1946 London audience, however, is likely to have contained men like Gerald. The stage direction therefore sets Gerald up as a character with whom some members of the audience will engage, sympathise with and finally condemn. Gerald is Priestley's tool to reveal the flaws of the upper classes.

First of all, Priestley reveals that Gerald's parents, Lord and Lady Croft, are unable to attend his engagement party; this confirms Gerald's role as a member of the upper classes. The absence of his parents suggests perhaps that they disapprove of the match. The audience might initially assume that Gerald wants to marry Sheila because he is madly in love with her; however, there are references throughout the play to his absences during the summer, which makes the audience wonder about him. We discover that Sheila was right to be concerned when we learn about his affair with Eva Smith. So, why is he marrying Sheila? We can only assume that, as the son of a successful businessman and aristocrat, there are business opportunities for Crofts Limited and Birling & Co., which Mr Birling references in his engagement speech and with which Gerald agrees ('Hear, hear!'). We therefore suspect that Gerald has business focused reasons for marriage—he is deceitful to Sheila, and he prioritises business over love.

Gerald very much allies himself with Mr Birling in business matters and, like Mr Birling, he initially denies knowing Eva Smith. His attitude is dismissive when he says 'I don't come into this suicide business'. The phrase 'suicide business' is cold-hearted and unexpected. Suicide is not a business in the sense that Crofts Limited is a business; however, 'business' can also mean a difficult matter or a scandalous event. By using the phrase 'suicide business', Priestley positions Gerald as superior because he implies that others are responsible for Eva's death. His reaction soon changes when he hears Eva Smith referred to as Daisy Renton, however, so Priestley positions the audience, which has seen his smug, aloof, self-assured confidence, to enjoy his discomfort in his pending interrogation.

Like Eric, Gerald considers the women who frequent the Palace Theatre bar only in terms of their appearance, and criticises their 'dough face[s]' and 'hard eye[s]'. This reveals how the commodification of women is totally normal for him. His complimentary description of Eva Smith's 'big dark eyes' reveals an attitude of objectification of her. He considers the women in the bar as if he is choosing an item in a shop—rather than thinking of her as a person, he is thinking of her as something for him to enjoy. He describes himself as saving Eva Smith from Joe Meggarty, but the truth is he was not much better himself.

When the inspector uncovers Gerald's affair with Eva, Priestley shows that Gerald is upset by her death. He reports ending the affair, saying 'She didn't blame me at all. I wish to God she had now'. Priestley here focuses the attention of the audience on what appears to be genuine remorse and self-blame. This makes the audience feel some sympathy towards him as a character and, for a while, the audience believes that Gerald will align himself with the inspector's views of social responsibility. This is particularly exciting, as he is a member of a class that holds power and has lots of social contacts in the higher echelons of society.

However, the audience changes its opinion of Gerald when in Act 3, he does everything that he can to prove that the inspector is a fake. Unlike Sheila and Eric, he has learnt nothing at all. Like Mr and Mrs Birling, he wants to avoid a public scandal and to protect himself and his wealth. At this point in the play, Priestley sets the audience up to condemn Gerald, particularly when he offers Sheila the engagement ring, saying 'Everything's all right now'. The audience sees that he has learnt absolutely nothing. Even if Eva does not exist, he refuses to reflect upon his treatment of Daisy Renton and to become a better person.

To conclude, for a moment, Priestley encourages the audience to sympathise with Gerald, in the hope that he (and the aristocracy he represents) will become a better person. When this fails to happen, the disappointed audience condemns him and his attitude towards Eva and, by default, towards vulnerable members of society. Through Gerald, Priestley presents the aristocracy as self-interested people who, instead of sharing their wealth, are more likely to follow family tradition of preserving it for the next generation.

Inspector Goole

In the 1938 edition of Theatre Arts Monthly, JB Priestley explains that the inspiration for one of his plays should be 'an idea that you could express very simply in five or ten words'. In 'An Inspector Calls', Inspector Goole best sums up the message of the play in two sentences: 'We are members of one body. We are responsible for each other'. Priestley uses the inspector as a mouthpiece for his socialist views: he is there to teach the Birling family, Gerald and the audience that we need to look out for each other, rather than focus solely on our own selfish ambitions and desires. Priestley uses many different techniques to present this simple message.

Maggie B Gale, in her book 'J.B. Priestley', states that Priestley 'wanted a social and political shift which took Britain forward to a society based on equality and community after the Second World War'. Priestley encourages his audience to examine their views by inverting generic expectations. 'An Inspector Calls' is a work of detective fiction, and Inspector Goole is the intelligent detective who will solve the case. A traditional detective story focuses on the narrowing down from a list of numerous suspects to just one, but Inspector Goole does the opposite and shows that everyone is responsible for the death of Eva Smith or, as he states shortly before his exit, 'each of you helped to kill her'. Priestley inverts the generic expectations of detective fiction to present the key message of social responsibility.

As well as inverting the detective genre, Priestley promotes his message of collective responsibility through sentence structure. Shortly after his arrival on stage in Act 1, Inspector Goole tells Mr Birling:

'Because what happened to her then may have determined what <u>happened to her afterwards</u>, and <u>what happened to her afterwards</u> may have driven her to suicide. A chain of events.'

Here we see an example of anadiplosis (underlined), where the second clause in the sentence begins by repeating the last words of the previous clause. As my good friend Tom Briars-Delve points out:

> Soon after his entrance, the audience start to realise that the inspector's investigation focuses on the surprising links between different events and people. The inspector initiates this idea of connections through anadiplosis; by repeating 'what happened to her afterwards' at the end of one clause and the beginning of the next, the sentence structure itself cleverly emphasises how the content of these statements is inextricably connected and leads on from one another.

So, the inversion of the expected generic conventions of the detective genre, coupled with the use of anadiplosis, hammer home the point that everyone's actions are interconnected, and all are responsible for the death of Eva Smith.

Briars-Delve continues:

> Next, Priestley memorably summarises this concept with the metaphorical image of 'A 'chain of events'. The concrete noun 'chain' refers to an object that embodies physical linking. Even more so than that, however, it connotes heaviness and imprisonment, perhaps inferring that the links between various 'events' involving the Birlings and Eva Smith could be what weighs down the entire family.
>
> Alternatively, chains can be broken, perhaps symbolising Priestley's hope that members of society can change their views about social responsibility and break the chains of a capitalist mindset.

Priestley also uses stage directions to signify the importance of Inspector Goole and the message he will bring. As Inspector Goole arrives, the stage directions at the start of Act 1 suggest the lighting should change from 'pink and intimate' to 'brighter and harder'. The 'pink and intimate' lighting symbolises the overly optimistic way the characters view themselves and their lives. They view life through rose tinted glasses, seeing things as better than they truly are. They are, as another of the opening stage directions informs us 'pleased with themselves'. With the arrival of the inspector comes the change of lighting to 'brighter and harder'. This shift signifies a number of changes. To begin with, the lighting becomes harsh and intense, mirroring the lighting of an interrogation: each character is placed under the spotlight. The lighting shift would also illuminate every part of the stage—every nook and cranny, every corner is now illuminated, symbolising how Inspector Goole's presence will illuminate the dark parts of each character's life.

And what about the inspector himself? Priestley deliberately portrays the inspector as a mysterious character. For a playwright who goes into great detail in some stage directions (for example, the opening page of the play is almost entirely made up of stage direction), Priestley tells us very little about Inspector Goole. Even the inspector's dialogue reveals what he is not, rather than what he is: 'I don't play golf' and 'I never take offence'. This vagueness of character is deliberate on the part of Priestley, as it creates a sense of ambiguity and mystery. This is added to by the character's name. It is often noted that the inspector's name, 'Goole' sounds like the word 'ghoul', meaning ghost or spirit, and it is true that the inspector does haunt Gerald and the Birlings about their role in Eva's death. It is also true that the inspector at times seems to know too much about a girl who died two hours ago, even though he has read her letter and 'sort of diary'. This has led some to wonder if the inspector is a supernatural being. There is no definitive answer either way about the inspector's identity: he might be an imposter or a supernatural being. But one thing is clear: descriptions are deliberately vague and ambiguous. This helps the audience to focus less on the character himself and more on the message he brings. And that message is loudly declared with no subtlety whatsoever.

With most of Inspector Goole's dialogue, Priestley uses questions: he interrogates the characters on stage, which is exactly what we would expect from a detective investigating a crime. However, at times, Goole delivers lines of dialogue that seem to come directly from the mouth of Priestley, hammering home the message of social responsibility that he wants the audience to learn. Examples include:

'it would do us all a bit of good if sometimes we tried to put ourselves in the place of these young women'

'we have to share something. If there's nothing else, we'll have to share our guilt.'

'We often do on the young ones. They're more impressionable.'

'Public men…have responsibilities as well as privileges.'

And of course, in the inspector's long final speech, which some members of the audience might consider melodramatic, believing that Priestley uses too much hyperbole (exaggeration). Priestley uses the inspector to speak directly to the audience, and the playwright's lack of subtlety led Sewell Stoke, in his 1947 Theatre Arts article Panache and Port Wine to write: 'Then the bell rings and in comes Inspector Goole (Inspector Priestley, to be more exact)'. The character of Inspector Goole does seem to be the embodiment of JB Priestley himself—a mouthpiece used to hammer home the socialist message that he wants the audience to take home with them.

Priestley took this educational value of the theatre very seriously. In the January 1938 Theatre Arts Monthly, Priestley is asked: 'If there was a theme that affected you profoundly, one that you felt it all-important to record before you died, what medium would you choose to express it?' He answers: 'If I wanted to make people feel deeply, I should use the drama. You can create a quality of emotion in the theatre beyond any you can achieve in another medium.' It is important to know that Priestley was also a very successful novelist. Therefore, he deliberately chose to write plays to present important messages. Here, we see that his important message is most clearly articulated through the character of Inspector Goole.

Priestley enhances his message through his use of supernatural imagery in the inspector's final words about 'fire and blood and anguish'. This is an allusion to the Biblical description of hell being a 'blazing furnace, where there will be weeping and gnashing of teeth' (Matthew 13:42). However, Priestley's point here cannot accurately be labelled as Biblical. His message seems to be that people need to do good deeds to make their way into heaven, and those who do not, will end up in hell. This is a moralistic concept that is not found in the Bible. The Bible says that faith in Jesus gets you to heaven, and good works come as a result of that faith, rather than being the entry ticket into heaven. Either way, the Biblical language adds to the supernatural, other-worldly aspect of Inspector Goole, which helps us to so clearly remember his message. This imagery of 'fire and blood and anguish' can also be interpreted as foreshadowing the pain and suffering of the two world wars which would soon follow the historical setting of the play. The contemporary audience would be fully aware of the 'fire and blood and anguish' of WW1 and WW2, and this adds to the sense of mystery surrounding Goole: how exactly does he know so clearly what is to follow? Knowing that Goole was right adds credibility to his ideas about socialism, just as knowing Birling was wrong about the Titanic and Germans wanting war is used to undermine his capitalist agenda. Priestley also employs syndetic listing in this quotation, (repeating the word 'and') to slow down the pace and allow each word in the list to have greater impact on the audience.

Through Priestley's presentation of the inspector, he calls upon the audience to change themselves and also encourage others to change. The power Inspector Goole wields is not something that comes from within himself or from his birthright (like the physical strength of Eric when he threatens to make a row, or the money Birling has, or the social status that comes from being born with a surname of the gentry). Instead, Inspector Goole's power comes from the way he can make others feel. It is because of this—his power is ordinary and could be obtained by anyone who is persistent in doing the right thing—that we can all aspire to be like him.

Minor Characters
Charlie Brunswick

Charlie Brunswick is a character mentioned only once, by Gerald, as he begins his confession to Inspector Goole about his involvement with Daisy Renton (Eva Smith).

Priestley uses Charlie Brunswick to portray Brumley as a town where the affluent seem to have exclusive access to the very best that the town has to offer. Charlie Brunswick 'had gone off to Canada for six months' and whether this was for business or pleasure, the casual use of 'gone off' implies that Gerald considers this sort of travel insignificant. This shows how worldly and privileged Gerald and Charlie are in comparison to Eva Smith who, in contrast, has only moved from the countryside to Brumley, and then got as far as the seaside before returning again. These geographical spheres of movement are important because they reveal just how limited the working class were in terms of their experience of the world. In both 1947 and 1912, any sort of international travel for the working class would have been unheard of—thus adding to the disproportionate power dynamic between Gerald and Eva, and generally between the upper classes and the working poor. It was Gerald needing to go away on business that prompted him to finish the relationship with Eva, presumably because it was no longer easy and convenient for him to continue the affair.

Charlie Brunswick also symbolises how the upper classes collectively benefit from a mass of wealth through their networking opportunities. Just as Birling attempts to use his relationship with Chief Constable Colonel Roberts as leverage at the beginning of Inspector Goole's investigation, Gerald is able to use Charlie Brunswick's vacant city property to benefit his own private affair. Priestley uses this presentation of privileged connections to juxtapose that of the working class: Eva Smith, whose 'parents were dead', had 'no home to go back to' and had 'few friends'.

Joe Meggarty

Joe Meggarty, the drunken womaniser who is behaving lecherously towards Eva Smith when Gerald first meets her, plays another important albeit minor role in the play. First of all, his character reveals the hypocrisy of some gentleman in Brumley, whose behaviour in private is a mismatch to their behaviour in public. For example, Mrs Birling is shocked to learn that he is a 'notorious womanizer' and 'one of the worst sots and rogues'. According to Sheila, 'everybody knows', revealing to the audience that Mrs Birling's ignorance is therefore chosen. If she does not look, she does not have to know, and this deliberate 'blindness' to the truth allows such behaviour to continue. When she questions the validity of the claim, Mrs Birling asks 'surely you don't mean Alderman Meggarty?'. This use of the title 'Alderman' focuses the attention of the audience on his status: as 'Alderman', he is in a position of authority and trust in the town, able to wield significant power and influence in terms of what can be done. In contrast, Eva had her job taken away from her for just asking for more money—something that Birling and Meggarty as businessmen would do all the time.

Priestley also uses Meggarty to highlight how oblivious Gerald is to his own behaviour. Gerald's pronouncement of disgust at Meggarty's behaviour demonstrates a total lack of insight into how Gerald's own behaviour might be perceived. Where Gerald sees a 'womanizer' in Meggarty, he fails to see he is just the same, and this demonstrates an inability to consider the wider impact of his behaviour. Even if Gerald did have genuine feelings for Eva, the fact is that he (and Eric) went to the Palace Variety Theatre bar, knowing it was 'a favourite haunt of women of the town'. Men like Eric and Gerald went there to take advantage of the poverty and desperation of lower-class women. Even the phrasing of 'favourite haunt' places the action upon the sex workers, as if it is them who are picking favourites and doing their job out choice rather than necessity. This further demonstrates a total disconnect between Gerald's actions and the feelings of the women whom he abuses.

The **Leaders of Strike Action at Birling & Co.** The women who headed up the strike at Birling's factory have a significant role in the play. Trade Union law now protects workers from being sacked as Eva Smith was. From 1912 to 1945, trade union membership grew, and workers fought for more power. Priestley uses Mr Birling's unreasonable reaction to the strike action as an example of the short-sightedness of capitalists who created difficult working conditions for the working classes. Instead of working with his employees, Mr Birling instead dismisses the ringleaders and Eva Smith. Although we learn of Eva Smith's downfall into poverty, the audience does not forget that there are the unknown stories of the other ringleaders, later alluded to when Inspector Goole declares that there are 'millions and millions' of Eva Smiths and John Smiths. The ambiguity of the factory work is also an important symbol in the play—Priestley is intimating that this story could happen anywhere, to anyone. This is therefore not industry specific, and his speech is all about the power the rich have over the poor.

The End of the Play: Unanswered Questions

There are unanswered questions and unresolved issues at the end of 'An Inspector Calls', as well as different possible interpretations of the ending. Some audience members may be frustrated that it is not entirely clear whether Inspector Goole was a real police inspector; whether Eva and Daisy are the same person; and whether the Birling family did actually contribute to a young woman's death. It is therefore important to examine why Priestley might have chosen to leave some of these questions unanswered.

Was Inspector Goole real?
Ultimately, it does not matter whether Inspector Goole was real or not. Priestley leaves this question unanswered because he wants the audience to focus on the actions and words of the characters, regardless of the outcome.

Does it matter if you commit a crime but do not get caught? Does it matter if you do not feel guilty? Or take any responsibility? Priestley, using the inspector as his mouthpiece, believes it does matter.

The whole point is that Eva was unfairly sacked in the first place. Whether the inspector was real is not relevant. Priestley, a socialist, is suggesting that the lesson to be learned is one of social responsibility. We should take responsibility for our behaviour towards others because this is the right thing to do.

What is the significance of the Photograph he carries?
Who is in the inspector's photograph or photographs? Are Eva and Daisy the same person? The photographs are a device to prompt the audience (and the characters) to consider whether Eva and Daisy are the same person and whether each character has, in some way, mistreated the same person. The characters sometimes try and see the photograph, but the inspector never allows it, always controlling the situation and making them wait their turn. In between these turns, he puts the picture or pictures in his pocket.

It is Gerald, near the end of the play, who questions whether or not the inspector is real and whether or not they have all been being questioned about a different young woman. Eric and Sheila remain distraught. It does not matter to them whether Goole is actually a real inspector and whether they have all been talking about the same person. They both recognise their wrongdoings and take responsibility for their actions. In contrast, Mr and Mrs Birling see the possibilities of a hoax as a way of avoiding the situation and any guilt they may be feeling over their actions.

Eric never reveals the name of the girl he met, and Mrs Birling only knew the young woman by the name she called herself, 'Mrs Birling'. It is possible that they all met a different person, but ultimately it makes no difference, as they still treated a young woman in the way they did.

Priestley's point is that the Birlings and Gerald Croft behaved badly towards a young working-class woman: it does not matter if it was the same woman.

It also does not matter if they were part of a 'chain of events' or not. Priestley believes that we all need to take responsibility for our actions and look after one another. The inspector makes this message clear in his final speech when he says 'We are members of one body. We are responsible for each other'.

What's the Significance of the Telephone Call at the very End of the Play?
Towards the end of the play, the tension drops when the characters learn that there is no Inspector Goole in the Brumley police force and no-one has been taken to the Infirmary, having committed

suicide by drinking disinfectant. Then the tension rapidly rises with the final telephone call, and the audience is left on a cliff hanger.

This structure could be frustrating for some members of the audience, so it is essential to consider why Priestley might have chosen to end his play in this way. In the inspector's final speech, he predicts 'fire and blood and anguish'. Priestley suggests that people have the choice to learn the inspector's lesson of social responsibility. If they refuse to help others and remain very selfish in their approach to life, they will not get away with it. The words 'fire, and blood and anguish' could refer to war. If people refuse to accept responsibility for anyone other than themselves, this attitude could end in the horror of war. Alternatively, it may mean they will have to pay the price in the afterlife as 'fire and blood and anguish' are all words associated with Hell.

Even though Eric, Sheila and to some extent Gerald accept responsibility for their actions during the course of the play, Mr and Mrs Birling do not. The final phone call—in which the Birlings learn that a young woman has died after drinking disinfectant and a police inspector is on his way—supports the ideas proposed by the inspector in his final speech.

We cannot escape his lesson of social responsibility.

Men and women will be forced to learn that lesson one way or another. Sure enough, the Birlings are to be questioned again and will have to face the consequences of their actions.

Is the Play really about the Birlings?
It is important to remember that the play is socialist propaganda. Therefore, all the characters in the play, as we have seen in the character analysis of this guide, are stereotypes, symbolising aspects of Edwardian society.

The Birlings represent the wealthy in society; Priestley criticises them as selfish people, concerned primarily with money and their reputations. Eric and Sheila show that young people are, as the inspector says, more 'impressionable'. They are capable of learning the lesson of social responsibility and changing their ways. This offers hope to the post-war audience who were trying to rebuild their future. If we educate young people, they are the ones who will create a better society.

Mr and Mrs Birling represent the older, wealthier citizens who are equally selfish and capable of being cruel, but who are more entrenched in their ways. Due to this, Priestley may well be proposing that we focus on the education of young people. If we make them realise the need to take responsibility for their actions, this will be more effective than wasting time on people who are far less likely to change.

Although he is not technically a member of the Birling family, we should also consider Gerald Croft. For a short time, he appears to be sorry for the way he has treated Eva, providing hope that he will side with the younger generation and adopt the inspector's socialist views. By the end of the play, he has aligned himself more to the views of the older Birlings. Like them, he has an interest in retaining his wealth. As a member of the upper class, his wealth will be inherited. It is therefore in his interest to keep it and pass it to the next generation.

Eva represents the working class, not only women but men too. As the Inspector says, 'One Eva Smith has gone—but there are millions and millions and millions of Eva Smiths and John Smiths still left with us'. Priestley wants to make us realise that there are many people alive and suffering in our society. We should help them, rather than just focusing on our own lifestyle and gains in a selfish way. (See the character of Eva Smith for further analysis of her role in the play.)

Rather than being a play about Eva, the Birlings and Gerald, the play can be seen as a vehicle for Priestley to deliver his socialist views via the character of Inspector Goole. As we have already seen, the inspector is the mouthpiece of Priestley, who makes us aware that 'Public men...have responsibilities as well as privileges'.

What is Priestley's main Message in the Play? Is there anything I must include in an analytical Essay?

It is hard to see how an essay could be written about 'An Inspector Calls' without including Priestley's message of social responsibility. This is explored further in the themes chapter of this guide.

The Opening Stage Directions: An Analysis

The length of the opening stage directions in 'An Inspector Calls' reflects their importance. They not only introduce the Birling family, but they also introduce key themes in the play.

Our first hint of tension in the family is with Priestley's description of the dining-room as 'heavily comfortable but not cosy and homelike'. Priestley uses the oxymoron 'heavily comfortable' to hint at unease. The adjective 'heavily' implies force, effort and weight. However, the adjective 'comfortable' has two interpretations. The first is that the furniture is pleasant, enjoyable and easy to relax in; the second is that it is as large as it needs to be (think about a comfortable income). The jarring oxymoron implies that the furniture is expensive and bought to impress others, but that it is not easy to relax. This is reinforced with the words 'not cosy and homelike'. The room is for show, a way for the Birlings to display their rich lifestyle. This is one of the first hints of tension within the family: all is not as it first appears. It also introduces the theme of wealth—and of course, this links to later discussions about how money should be spent.

Priestley introduces the themes of capitalism and socialism through the lighting. Described as 'pink and intimate', it mirrors the mood of the characters at the start of the play. These adjectives connote romance and closeness, fitting for an engagement party. They also suggest, however, that the characters are looking at life through rose-tinted spectacles. In other words, they are happy with their lives, but they see things in a positive way, believing that life is better than it actually is. Certainly, when we first hear the family discussing Sheila and Gerald's engagement, it does seem as if they are happy and contented, oblivious to any of their recent poor behaviour. The lighting could therefore also symbolise the self-satisfaction of capitalism.

When the inspector arrives, the stage directions state that the lighting should change to 'brighter and harder'. It is as if the inspector has metaphorically come to shine a spotlight on the characters, shedding light on the 'chain of events' which led to the death of Eva Smith. The harshness and intensity of the lighting connotes an interrogation light, implying that the inspector will place each character under the spotlight, challenging their capitalist sense of entitlement and selfishness. Furthermore, the lighting shift will illuminate every part of the stage, symbolising how Inspector Goole's presence will illuminate the dark parts of each character's life. The playwright in turn encourages audience members to reflect on their own lives, after having been hopefully illuminated by his socialist ideas.

The theme of class is introduced with the reference to the Birlings' parlour maid, Edna. (A detailed analysis of her character has already been provided in the relevant character chapter.) Note her actions: she is clearing the table of 'champagne glasses' amongst other items, and replacing them with items such as a 'port' decanter and 'cigar box'—all expensive signifiers of wealth. These props, together with the character of Edna, again position the Birlings as a rich family who are keen to show off.

When studying the opening stage directions, it is important to consider how Priestley introduces characters because we can gain an insight into how he wants the audience to see them. A detailed analysis of each character is in the relevant character chapter, above. Let's see how much you remember! Here are the introductory key quotes for each character. Analyse them and then check your answers in the relevant character chapter:

Character	Quotation
Mr Birling	'heavy-looking, rather portentous man in his middle fifties with fairly easy manners but rather provincial in his speech.'
Mrs Birling	'cold' and Mr Birling's 'social superior'

Eric Birling	'half shy, half assertive'
Sheila Birling	'pretty girl in her early twenties, very pleased with life and rather excited'
Gerald Croft	'easy, well-bred young man-about-town'

It is interesting to note that Mr Birling seems to fit in with the room since he is 'heavy-looking' and the furniture is 'heavily comfortable'. Priestley implies that he, like his furniture, does not consider the comfort or wellbeing of others. This of course foreshadows what we later learn of his capitalist views, which prioritise himself and his family above all others.

Interestingly, the Birlings and Gerald Croft are all in evening dress, again showing the importance of outward appearances; perhaps Priestley is hinting that appearances and social status matter more to the family than their morals.

At the end of the stage directions, the characters are summed up as 'pleased with themselves'. The opening dialogue then reflects this mood: Sheila and Gerald are happy that they have become engaged; Mr Birling is delighted about the match because it might prove good for his business, and he talks about his hopes for a knighthood in the near future.

It is the subsequent arrival of Inspector Goole which interrupts the self-congratulatory mood of the Birlings with a 'sharp ring' of the doorbell.

The Inspector's Final Speech: An Analysis

Inspector Goole's parting words are very important, as they sum up the main message of the play. There are three key sections to consider.

Firstly, Priestley stresses that Eva Smith is actually a symbol, a representative of all poor and disadvantaged members of society. The inspector states 'One Eva Smith has gone—but there are millions and millions and millions of Eva Smiths and John Smiths still left with us'. By choosing the name 'Eva', which might be a Biblical reference to Eve the first woman, and combining it with the common surname 'Smith', Priestley emphasises that in Eva Smith symbolises all women. Therefore, Priestley does not want his audience to feel sorry for one working-class woman, but all working-class women. Furthermore, 'John' is a very common male name, so the inspector now repositions Eva as also representing working-class men, who are also victims of social injustice.

The playwright's use of syndetic listing (repeating the word 'and') slows down the pace and emphasises the repetition of 'millions' to reinforce the message that Eva's story has not finished with her death—there are other women and men who need support. It is essential that we all take responsibility for our actions towards others, including those less fortunate than ourselves.

This section is followed by possibly the most important words in the entire play: 'We don't live alone. We are members of one body. We are responsible for each other'. Priestley's use of the rule of three with the simple sentences emphasises his socialist message. His repetition of 'We' at the start of each sentence also stresses the importance of community and shared responsibility. **It is hard to imagine an exam answer which does not include these lines**. They sum up Priestley's message of social responsibility completely. Whether writing about characters, themes, structure, etc., you could include analysis of these lines, as the whole play revolves around the inspector (the mouthpiece of Priestley) delivering a message of social responsibility both to the Birlings and the audience.

The final part of the inspector's speech contains a warning for those unwilling to accept this lesson of social responsibility, and he predicts 'fire and blood and anguish'. The words 'fire and blood and anguish' have at least two possible interpretations. Firstly, they reference the Bible (see Inspector Goole character analysis), so one suggestion is that Priestley (via the inspector) is saying if we are unwilling to take responsibility for one another here on earth, then we will be sent to Hell to learn the lesson there ('fire' and 'anguish' certainly suggest Hell). This interpretation fits with the pun on the inspector's last name—a ghoul from the afterlife might be a messenger from God, sent to warn those on Earth of the consequences of their actions if they do not learn to take responsibility for their behaviour. Priestley's use of syndetic listing again slows the pace and allow each word in the list to have greater impact on the audience.

Alternatively, the words 'fire and blood and anguish' have connotations of war. The inspector may be telling the characters and the audience that, if men and women refuse to look after one another, more wars will follow. The play was first performed in 1945 after two world wars to an audience who had experienced one or both of them. The audience would therefore infer that the older Birlings and Gerald, representing the 1912 rich and selfish, did not learn their lesson, and this resulted in war. The situational irony of the inspector's words is therefore highly relevant to the audience. Knowing that Goole was right adds credibility to Priestley's ideas about socialism, just as knowing Birling was wrong about the Titanic and Germans wanting war undermines ideas about capitalism.

Age: Who accepts Responsibility and why?

There is no doubt that 'An Inspector Calls' presents a division between the younger characters, in particular Sheila and Eric, and the older characters of Mr and Mrs Birling. However, it would be an oversimplification to simply state that all began with the same mindset but the young learned the inspector's lesson whilst the old did not. The truth is that divisions were evident even before the arrival of the inspector.

Priestley uses slang and idiomatic language to symbolise the difference between young and old in the opening act of the play. In the opening three of four pages, Sheila tells Eric he is 'squiffy' (meaning drunk). Mrs Birling's reaction forces the audience to acknowledge the difference between young and old, 'What an expression, Sheila! Really, the things you girls pick up these days!' Seconds later, Sheila calls Eric a 'chump' (meaning idiot). Eric himself tells his father, shortly before the entrance of the inspector, that Mr Birling has 'piled it on a bit'. These examples of slang and idiomatic language indicate, before the arrival of the inspector, that there is a division to be noted between the young and old members of the Birling family. This division will ultimately lead to Eric and Sheila learning the valuable lesson the inspector brings, with Mr and Mrs Birling rejecting it.

Sheila and Eric, the youngest characters, both accept that they had a part to play in Eva Smith's death, and they clearly regret their actions. Their words and the stage directions both ensure their sorrow is clear. Sheila says 'I behaved badly…I'm ashamed of it', and the stage directions suggest she looks 'as if she's been crying'. Eric accepts responsibility when he says 'We did her in all right'. They do not change their views in Act 3 when they discuss the identity of the inspector. They still feel remorse, even when they first learn that no young woman has committed suicide and been admitted to the infirmary. It is clear that they have accepted responsibility for their actions.

Gerald is slightly older than Sheila and Eric, and he does accept some responsibility for his actions, particularly when he is being questioned by the inspector: 'She didn't blame me at all. I wish to God she had now'. Despite this, as the end of the play nears, he is keen to believe 'Everything's alright now'. He has not learnt anything from the evening's events, and he aligns himself more closely with the views of the older Birlings.

The greatest contrast in attitude can be seen between the siblings Sheila and Eric and their parents. Mr and Mrs Birling refuse to accept that they are even partly to blame for the tragedy. Mr Birling makes it clear: 'I can't accept any responsibility'. Near the end of the play, when the inspector's identity is brought into question, he insists (like Gerald) 'But the whole thing's different now'. Mrs Birling similarly refuses to feel guilty about her involvement: 'I told him quite plainly that I thought I had done no more than my duty'. They are entrenched in their views.

It is now important to consider why Priestley presents the audience with this distinction between the two generations. The inspector is the mouthpiece of Priestley, stating that 'young ones' are 'more impressionable'. When the younger characters learn the lesson of social responsibility, this suggests that there is some hope for the future. The younger generation can be taught to accept responsibility for one another; it is possible for them to change and, if they do, society will be a better place. This fits in neatly with Priestley's socialist views, including the emphasis he put on education as a way of changing society for the better. We must also not forget that, when the play was first performed, the audience members had just experienced World War II, so they would probably be keen to see a more compassionate society in which people take responsibility for their actions.

In your exam, if you are asked to write about the differences between the older and younger generations of the Birling family, remember that you will gain more marks by exploring your ideas and writing a lot about a little. For this reason, I recommend focusing your discussion one member of each generation, so that you give yourself enough time to pick apart quotes and ideas.

Key Themes

An overview of the main themes is below. When analysing themes, it is important to remember that Priestley's overarching message is one of social responsibility. In the words of the inspector, 'We are members of one body. We are responsible for each other'. An overview of the themes and how they link to the characters is below. For more detail, you should review the character chapters.

Class

Priestley uses the theme of class to draw the attention of the audience to divisions in 1912 society. As a socialist, Priestley wanted the audience to critically examine the pre-war class system and to consider how socialism could create a fairer society in which 'We are responsible for each other'. Capitalism, on the other hand was, he believed, divisive and exploited the working classes. The division in classes plays an important role in 'An Inspector Calls'. The Birling family and Gerald represent the wealthy middle and upper classes who exploit the working classes, represented by Eva Smith and Edna.

Priestley first draws our attention to the theme of class in the opening stage directions of the play. He hints that Mr Birling has worked his way up through the class system when we learn that he is 'provincial in his speech'. This implies that he was not born to money, and that he is a self-made man. The wealthy manufacturer appears to be highly conscious that socially, he is 'inferior'. He has made up for this with high profile public roles, which are a source of pride. He tells Gerald that he was 'Lord Mayor' and later, he tries to use his status to exert power over the inspector: 'I was an alderman for years—and I'm still on the Bench'. Priestley challenges ideas about social status through the inspector, who is quick to remind him that 'Public men...have responsibilities as well as privileges'.

Mr Birling's apparent obsession with rising further in the class system creates the impression of ruthless social climber. We suspect that he initially achieved some of his success by marrying Sybil, his 'social superior'. (He has also provided Eric with a public school and university education, ensuring that his son has the advantages that he did not.) We are aware that Mr Birling is pleased with Sheila's engagement although his reasons link more to ambition and business opportunities than his daughter's welfare: he hopes that, one day, the Crofts and Birlings will be 'working together—for lower costs and higher prices'. We assume that Gerald will one day inherit the title of Lord Croft, as there are no references to him having siblings. Sheila's social status would therefore rise too, as she would become Lady Sheila Croft. Priestley uses Mr Birling's attitude to social status to draw the attention of the audience to those in society who value their social standing above the welfare of others.

We suspect that Gerald's parents, Lord and Lady Croft, are not at their son's engagement party because they disapprove of him marrying Sheila, who is of a lower social status. However, Mr Birling is quick to tell Gerald that there is 'a very good chance of a knighthood'. Mr Birling's desire to become Lord Birling reveals his ambition to rise and his assumption that he would be accepted into the upper echelons of society. Indeed, once the truth about his (and his family's) involvement with Eva is revealed, Mr Birling is more worried about a public scandal than his contribution to the death of Eva.

Priestley uses Eric and Sheila to draw attention to the fact that the attitudes of young people towards the working classes can change. This represents hope for his socialist ideas.

The playwright uses Gerald to represent the upper classes. For a moment, it appears that Gerald will change his attitude to Eva when he is upset about her death. In Act 3, however, the audience, whose hopes have been raised, roundly condemns him when they see that he has not changed at all. Being a member of the upper classes, it is in his interest to keep his inherited wealth.

Finally, Priestley uses the characters of Eva Smith and Edna to draw attention to conditions for the working classes in 1912. For a detailed analysis, please see their character chapters.

Love and Relationships

Priestley uses relationships to draw attention to his socialist message by criticising capitalism. At the start of the play, he aligns Sheila's engagement to Gerald to capitalism. The couple seem happy enough at the start of the of the play, but the focus is on the match being beneficial for business reasons. Mr Birling hopes that, one day, the Crofts and Birlings will be 'working together—for lower costs and higher prices'. Priestley depicts their engagement as a business transaction to draw attention to Mr Birling's misguided priorities: like Mrs Birling, the audience would regard his speech as inappropriate. This in turn depicts Mr Birling with his capitalist values in a negative light, influencing the audience to dislike him.

We also have a hint of the engagement as a transaction because there is little mention of love between the Gerald and Sheila; in fact, she needs the engagement ring so she can really 'feel engaged'. It is almost as if she needs the security of a ritual. In 1912, middle-class women were expected to marry and have children. Their husbands were expected to provide for them—they were not expected or encouraged to have careers of their own (note that Mr Birling references a public school and university for Eric, but he will not have invested the same money in Sheila's education). Sheila therefore follows expected conventions for middle-class young women.

She also follows traditional roles and expectations when she asks Gerald about the ring: 'is it the one you wanted me to have?'. Priestley's use of the question shows that she is happy to accept a passive, subordinate role. (This point is developed in more detail in Sheila's character chapter.)

Priestley uses the engagement to hint at unease and tension between the couple when Sheila comments on 'last summer, when you never came near me, and I wondered what had happened to you'. This foreshadows what we will later learn of Gerald's affair with Eva, so their engagement is used by Priestley as a device to prepare the audience for later revelations.

When Sheila refuses to accept Gerald's engagement ring at the end of the play, this symbolises that she has rejected traditional capitalist values. Now more independently minded, she has rejected the traditional pathway of marriage (and by default, has rejected traditional ideas to do with capitalism) in favour of socialist ideas. Sheila now realises that there are options for the future that she should now consider ('I must think'). Like her brother, she is prepared to challenge the status quo in order to make society a better place.

Priestley uses the relationship between Mr and Mrs Birling to show the worst that capitalism can offer. Despite being a married couple, again there seems little affection between Mr and Mrs Birling. Mrs Birling is described as a 'cold' woman and her husband's 'social superior' at the start of the play. As discussed in the previous section, we suspect that Mr Birling married Sybil for the social advantages that the match would bring. The interesting question, however, is why she might have married him. Could she also have been motivated by money? Mr Birling, as we are aware, is wealthy. Despite their relationship appearing rather cold, they do share the same views on social responsibility. Neither character is prepared to take responsibility for the death of Eva Smith. The couple therefore represents Priestley's view that the older generation is selfish, fixed in its views and will not embrace socialist ideas.

Priestley uses Eva's relationship with Gerald and Eric to show the double standards of Edwardian society. As we have already discussed, middle- and upper-class men would expect to marry a virgin, but they thought nothing of exploiting young working-class women for their bodies. Both men met Eva at Palace Variety Theatre and both men say that she stood out from the other women in the bar—this implies that they had been there before to pick up women. Although there appears to have been some affection between Gerald and Eva, he thinks nothing of ending the relationship when it is no longer convenient. Priestley encourages the audience to pity Eva when we learn that she went to the seaside at the end of the relationship to think of Gerald in order to think about him. Likewise, Priestley positions Eva as a noble woman with a sense of morality when she refuses to accept Eric's money or offer of marriage. Through these relationships, Priestley show the audience how capitalist self-interest can exploit vulnerable young women who, like Eva, have no other way to survive in a society that lacks a welfare state. He also uses the relationships to challenge any stereotypical attitudes that audience members might have (attitudes that are similar to Mrs Birling's) about working-class women.

Selfishness

Priestley uses 'An Inspector Calls' as a vehicle to criticise capitalism, so it is unsurprising that selfishness is a key theme in the play. Mr Birling is depicted as selfish for focusing on his business and the profits it makes, rather than on the welfare of his workers. Eva went on strike for higher wages, but he sacked her without further thought. Similarly, Mr Birling is happy about Sheila's engagement to Gerald Croft because he can see how the connection could boost profits with the Crofts and Birlings 'working together—for lower costs and higher prices'. He is frequently concerned with his reputation and how his involvement in Eva's death might reflect on his chances of a knighthood. He is certainly selfish in his attitude and behaviour.

Like Mr Birling, Mrs Birling does not change her selfish attitude; she feels no pity towards Eva Smith, and Priestley uses Mrs Birling to highlight the need for a common welfare state. Through Mrs Birling, we see that the charity committee's decisions are made at the whim of influential people. Mrs Birling admits that she was 'prejudiced' against Eva, because she adopted the name Mrs Birling when she went to the committee to ask for help. Sybil Birling selfishly cares about her pride and social standing: she lacks compassion and does not consider (or care about) the impact her refusal of help will have on Eva. Sheila does show some compassion and regret for what happened, but Mrs Birling maintains her selfish attitude throughout the play. This suggests that in Priestley's view, the older generations are selfish and wrong in their capitalist complacency, prioritising their own needs above all others.

Priestley uses Sheila to show that people can change. Sheila can also be seen as selfish, as she was concerned only with her own feelings of jealousy when she realised that Eva looked better in a dress than she did during her trip to Milwards Department Store. She does, at least, realise the error of her ways as the play progresses: 'I behaved badly too. I know I did. I'm ashamed of it'. Her ability to change and think about the impact that her behaviour has on Eva shows that, in Priestley's opinion, the younger generation can mature into responsible citizens who recognise the need to consider the common good.

Similarly, Eric Birling changes. At the beginning of the play, he is also a selfish character. On the night he met Eva in the Palace Theatre bar, he forced his way into Eva's lodgings for sex. Again, he was only concerned with his feelings at the time and did not think of the longer term implications. He does, like Sheila, regret his actions and change his selfish views by the end of the play. By aligning themselves with Priestley's socialist ideas, the younger generation provides hope that society can become a better place.

Priestley deliberately manipulates the audience with the character of Gerald Croft. Like Eric, he selfishly used Eva for her body. Despite initially appearing to regret his actions, by the end of the play, it is clear that Gerald has learnt nothing. At the suggestion that Goole might not be a real inspector, he is quick to selfishly conclude 'Everything's alright now'. When the audience sees that he has not learnt his lesson, this dashes any hopes that his apparent change was permanent, making the audience criticise Gerald more harshly. In turn, the audience is more likely to judge the upper classes in society who have the power and connections to change society but choose not to.

Social Responsibility

The theme of social responsibility is easy to over-simplify in 'An Inspector Calls'. A basic approach would simply be to state that everyone is responsible for the death of Eva Smith, and so everyone needs to look out for others. However, the theme is presented in a number of complex ways, which we shall now explore in this chapter.

WHO IS THE MAIN CHARACTER?

One of the most intriguing aspects about 'An Inspector Calls' is the way in which there is no one main character in the play. Think about that for a second. Consider your Shakespeare play: who is the main character in that? In many Shakespeare plays it is the title character/s (Macbeth, Romeo and Juliet, Othello) who are the main characters, but would we say that Priestley's main character is the inspector? I doubt it. If nothing else, he enters late and leaves before the end of the play. This is Priestley's way of helping us to focus on the characters who start and end on-stage: Gerald and the Birlings. Think about your 19th Century novel – who is the main character there? Scrooge? Sherlock Holmes? Jekyll / Hyde? We take it for granted, but in 'An Inspector Calls' there really is no one key character, and that is deliberate on the part of JB Priestley.

Priestley went to great lengths to ensure that the focus of the play did not fall on one single character alone. If we could pin the entire tragedy on the stupidity of Mr Birling, for example, we as an audience would be let off the hook from the message it is supposed to leave with all of us. The message would apply simply to capitalist businessmen who make their money at the expense of poor treatment of workers. But the play is not all about Mr Birling: it's about everyone. How else did Priestley make sure the focus of the play was not on one character alone? Well, he inverted the generic expectations of detective fiction; directed perspective altering stage management, and used sentence structure to show that the message of the play rests on all characters, and therefore all audience members. We've explored some of this already in the character analyses, but let's go over the key points again.

GENERIC CONVENTIONS: DETECTIVE FICTION

It is possible to analyse 'An Inspector Calls' as a work of detective fiction. Those of you who study 'The Sign of Four' for your 19th Century novel will be aware of the generic conventions of detective fiction, and can probably see how 'An Inspector Calls' fulfils some of them. For example, the detective must be an intelligent character and an outsider to those involved in the case – so far so good with Inspector Goole. However, 'An Inspector Calls' can be seen to challenge one of the most common conventions of detective fiction.

Most detective stories begin with a number of suspects, and slowly narrow down that number to the one guilty criminal. You can think of the game Cluedo as an example, where the challenge is to use a process of elimination to work out the one actual criminal. However, 'An Inspector Calls' turns this process on its head, and can be seen as a new take on the genre of detective fiction. Rather than narrowing down suspects from a large group to one, Inspector Goole shows us how Gerald and each member of the Birling family have contributed to Eva's death. Why does Priestley do this? To make his point that society as a whole is responsible for the mistreatment of others.

So the inversion of the detective thriller is a very clever, and often overlooked, device being used by Priestley. However, Priestley also uses staging to get the message across that no one singular character is the main hero or villain of the piece.

STAGING

It is impossible to read 'An Inspector Calls' without taking note of the large amount of stage directions present in the text. By far the most detailed of these comes at the start of the play, where the stage directions fill the entire first page of the text. Much has been said, including in this book, about the more obvious stage directions such as the change of lighting from 'pink and intimate' to 'brighter and harder', but there are more subtle, nuanced points which are also worthy of analysis.

Although the entire play takes place in one room, the opening stage directions in the text suggest two possible methods for staging. The first involves rearranging the props, furniture and characters after each act. This meant that the audience would appear to see the same drawing room but from a different angle for each act. The effect of this would be that a character who was facing the audience in Act One, might not be in Act Two. A character who had their back to the audience in Act Two, might be facing the audience in Act Three. In reality, this stage management – to rearrange the furniture, props and characters between acts, to view the room from a different perspective, would be very difficult to execute. Priestley knew this and so added a second option for a producer who wished to avoid the 'tricky business' of staging in such a way.

The question then, is WHY did Priestley write such a complicated set of stage directions, knowing how difficult they would be to execute? Well, the movement forcefully changes the audience's perspective of events. Just as we see how each different character has a different perspective of and role in the death of Eva, the staging forces us to see things from different perspectives too. As a result, again there is no one single character who remains front and centre for the entire play – the staging refuses to allow us to pick out one character to focus on: it forces us to see how all of the characters are responsible for the death of Eva.

Finally, Priestley uses sentence structure to get the message across that everyone is jointly responsible for the death of Eva, as reflected in the playwright's use of anadiplosis (thank you to Tom Briars-Delve for this following analysis of anadiplosis).

Anadiplosis is a clever name for beginning a sentence / clause by repeating the last word/s of the previous sentence/clause. We see an example when Inspector Goole says:

'Because what happened to her then may have determined <u>what happened to her afterwards</u>, and <u>what happened to her afterwards</u> may have driven her to suicide. A chain of events.'

Soon after his entrance, the audience start to realise that the inspector's investigation focuses on the surprising links between different events and people. The inspector initiates this idea of connections through anadiplosis; by repeating 'what happened to her afterwards' at the end of one clause and the beginning of the next, the sentence structure itself cleverly emphasises how the content of these statements is inextricably connected and leads on from one another. Again, the message is clear: no single person is responsible. No single person should be singled out. All are to blame. Next, he memorably summarises this concept with the metaphorical image of 'A chain of events'. The concrete noun 'chain' refers to an object that embodies physical linking. Even more so that that, however, it connotes heaviness and imprisonment, perhaps inferring that the links between various 'events' involving the Birlings and Eva Smith could be what weighs down the entire family.

So what we have is the inversion of the expected generic conventions of the detective thriller; the use of anadiplosis and the staging of the play, all used to hammer home the point that everyone's actions are interconnected and all are responsible for the death of Eva: very clever!

Another thing to consider is the variety of causes for the death of Eva Smith. As we have explored in the chapter on form, the various faults of the characters can be linked to the seven deadly sins.

The idea of there being 'seven deadly sins' is not a Biblical idea. It was a medieval creation suggesting that certain sins lead to death and others did not. However, the Bible's teaching on sin is that 'all have sinned and fall short of the glory of God' (Romans 3:23) and no sin is greater than another. With this in mind, the seven deadly sin analysis, whilst interesting, cannot accurately be viewed as Biblical imagery like the 'fire and blood and anguish' quote which certainly is Biblical (and is explored in the character analysis of Inspector Goole). More accurately, we can explore the wide range of 'sins' demonstrated as evidence that the play is aiming to challenge as many members of the audience as possible. The insinuation is that each member of the audience will be challenged by at least one of the characters' actions which they can relate to.

Stretch and Challenge: Other Interpretations

Important note: As was pointed out in the 2019 AQA report on the exam, critical theories should only be used in an exam answer if they enhance your interpretation of a text. You should not merely 'bolt on' comments about Marxism, Freud, feminism etc.

1. The Unities

Another way of analysing the structure of 'An Inspector Calls' derives is to consider The Unities of drama. The Ancient Greek philosopher Aristotle said that a play must conform to the following three unities:

Unity of Time

Action should take place within a single day. Ideally, the events in the play (stage time) happen in real time. We see this in the play when Act 2 continues from Act 1, and Act 3 continues from Act 2. This adds a sense of realism to the play, as the audience experiences events unfolding at the same time as the characters. This helps to hammer home Priestley's socialist message.

Unity of Place

There is just one setting. 'An Inspector Calls' is set in the Birlings' dining-room. This helps to focus the attention of the audience more fully.

Unity of Action

The plot has just one main storyline. Up until the inspector's exit, the storyline is driven by the inspector as he questions each character about their role in the death of Eva Smith. This makes the play easier for the audience to follow, and they are more likely to reflect on the ideas within the play.

When the audience sees events unfolding at the same time as the Birlings, Priestley encourages them to think about the character of the inspector, who comes across as omniscient. This is particularly the case when he says 'We often do on the young ones. They're more impressionable.' The audience immediately wants to know who the 'We' is, and this adds to the mystery of his character. Another example is at the end of Act 2 when the inspector mysteriously knows the exact moment that Eric will return. We do not know if the mysterious inspector is a human or a supernatural being. Ultimately, it does not matter. This is a conclusion that Sheila and Eric reach when they discuss whether he was a real police inspector. By applying the three unities when it suits him, Priestley creates a sense of mystery and focuses the attention of the audience more strongly on the character of the inspector and his socialist message.

2. The Greek Chorus

A Greek Chorus in Classical Greek drama was a group of masked actors who described and summarised events, commenting on events and characters in a play. In 'An Inspector Calls', Inspector Goole takes the role of the Greek Chorus—we might even say that he is Priestley, wearing the mask of the inspector. Priestley/the inspector summarises the 'chain of events' surrounding Eva's life, comments on the characters' behaviour and, with his exit speech, explains what lesson they need to learn.

3. Marxist Interpretation

Important note: As was pointed out in the 2019 AQA report on the exam, critical theories should only be used in an exam answer if they enhance your interpretation of a text. You should not merely 'bolt on' comments about Marxism, Freud, feminism etc.

Marxism is a political ideology based on the ideas of the founding fathers of communism, German political philosophers Karl Marx and Friedrich Engels. In 1848, they published their thoughts in The Communist Manifesto, a philosophical framework that aimed to create a classless society.

Marx and Engels argued that the aim of a capitalist society is to make a profit. It does not aim to help the weak and vulnerable. From a Marxist perspective, Mr Birling with his focus on 'lower costs and higher prices' symbolises the bourgeoisie: he is the capitalist exploiter of the working-classes, the proletariat, who are valued only for their labour. Eva Smith represents the overworked, underpaid proletariat, exploited by a capitalist master or, in the case of 'An Inspector Calls', all the characters who were initially aligned to capitalist values.

In order to achieve social change, Marx and Engels proposed a new economic and social system in which the state owns all property and resources on behalf of everyone. Marx believed that the only way to achieve this is through a revolution: 'The proletarians [common workers] have nothing to lose but their chains. They have a world to win. Workers of the world, Unite!'. We can almost hear the inspector's rallying call in his exit speech when he predicts 'fire and blood and anguish' if the characters do not heed his message of social responsibility.

Marxist theory argues that capitalism generates the conditions from which class warfare begin. We see this in the play when Eva Smith helps to organise a strike at Birling & Co. We also see this through Priestley's use of dramatic irony when Mr Birling references the 1912 Miners' Strike and says they are past the worst of it. The audience would know that the General Strike, in which more than one and a half million people went on strike, took place in 1926. There is more class conflict with the character of the inspector, who openly challenges the Birlings and Gerald about their treatment of Eva.

In 'An Inspector Calls', you will be referring to Priestley or the inspector's socialist message. It is worth taking a moment to understand the difference between socialism and communism because these are often confused. According to Marxist theory, a socialist state is a state that is in transition: it has overthrown capitalism but has not yet fully achieved communism. Communism applies to a society in which property is owned by the community rather than individuals. Each person is equal, contributing according to their ability and receiving according to their needs.

It is also important to consider contemporary British attitudes to the idea of socialism. After World War II in 1945, the Labour Party was voted into power. This is because its leader, Clement Attlee, had campaigned to make the country a better place by building affordable houses, providing full employment, creating a welfare state and a national health service. These are all socialist ideas. In 1912, socialist ideology was popular amongst writers like George Bernard Shaw and HG Wells (who Birling dismisses immediately after his speech laden with dramatic irony). In the eyes of the world, the Soviet Union was a successful, thriving Communist state, which, in the years that followed World War II, would begin its expansion into Eastern Europe (by 1949, it controlled all Eastern European governments except Yugoslavia).

Priestley was well aware that a play that promoted Marx's socialist ideology and attacked capitalism would be very well received in communist Russia. This is why he sent his script of 'An Inspector Calls' to Moscow where the play was first performed in 1945. The Soviet audience would have been amused by Priestley's use of dramatic irony with Mr Birling's prediction that Russia (i.e. the Russian Empire as it was called in 1912) would be 'behindhand'.

What was less obvious to the world was the human cost of change, which was covered up by the Soviet Union's propaganda machine. For example, in 1928, Stalin initiated a series of Five-Year Plans to modernise the Soviet Union, revitalising industry and agriculture. By centralising command of the economy and industrialisation, Stalin transformed the Soviet Union into an industrial power; however, the process of change caused huge suffering to the Russian people, disrupting food production. This resulted in a famine between 1932-3 in which it is estimated that 20 million people died.

As a result of the Five-Year Plans, by 1937 there were significant improvements in the production of coal, oil, iron and electricity, but conditions for the workers were still very bad.

Stalin, the General Secretary of the Communist Party also instigated the Great Purges, also known as the Great Terror, which took place in the late 1930s. Stalin removed anyone he considered disloyal (including senior military and political figures) by putting them on trial, torturing them until they made false admissions of guilt and then executing them. Other opponents were exiled internally to Siberia or put to work in brutal prison camps. 1939 was the climax of the Great Terror, which by this stage was targeting ordinary people. Having eliminated all internal opposition, Stalin became a totalitarian dictator. While the west was aware of the trials of Soviet leaders, the experiences of ordinary people were not reported or believed. In France, there were even attempts to discredit or silence witnesses; other Western observers simply could not see through the false charges and evidence.

The British public was therefore largely unaware that the reality of living under a communist regime was very different to the ideology voiced by Priestley/the inspector. This is partly because of the effectiveness of the Soviet propaganda machine in controlling information. It is also partly because the British press did not criticise the Soviet Union, which was at the time a war ally. For this reason, publishers initially refused to publish George Orwell's Animal Farm, a novella that criticised the hypocrisy of communism.

Nevertheless, in a communist country, workers have rights to which Eva did not have access because the focus of the ideology is on people rather than profits. These rights include:

- A decent wage
- The right to join a union
- The right to sue an employer for unfair dismissal e.g. being sacked because a customer had made a complaint based on anger and jealously

A Marxist interpretation of 'An Inspector Calls' is:

- Socialism makes people behave better. For example, Eva refuses to take stolen money and refuses Eric's offer of marriage.
- Socialism helps you to mature into a better person. For example, Sheila and Eric become better people because they embrace the inspector's socialist ideas.
- Capitalism makes people behave worse. Examples:
  - Mr Birling says he would offer 'thousands' to buy his family's way out of trouble and make things right after he learns that Eric has stolen money; he prioritises his reputation and avoiding a scandal. He did not consider giving 'thousands' Eva and his employees to make their lives better.
  - Mr and Mrs Birling do not change their views about capitalism. If we consider Marxist theory of sharing wealth, we understand that these characters would want to retain their wealth because they have the most to lose. (This would also apply to Gerald, who represents the aristocratic elite.)

From a Marxist perspective, Mr Birling therefore represents a capitalist society in which those in power are ignorant of the needs of the bourgeoisie and are unwilling to help them. Priestley therefore uses the character of Eva Smith to show that we should invest more in people and think less about profit: if we abolish the class system and share wealth, society will become a better place.

Freudian Interpretation

Important note: As was pointed out in the 2019 AQA report on the exam, critical theories should only be used in an exam answer if they enhance your interpretation of a text. You should not merely 'bolt on' comments about Marxism, Freud, feminism etc.

Sigmund Freud (1856-1939) is the founder of psychoanalysis, a method of treating patients through dialogue.

Freud's dreams theory is the idea that dreams reflect inner desires. These might be daydreams or dreams when sleeping. If we view the play through the lens of Freud's dreams theory, a psychoanalytical interpretation might be that the inspector is a manifestation (the embodiment of an abstract idea) of the characters' inner guilt.

Freud believed that the human personality (psyche) has three parts:

Id—instincts. This is the subconscious part of the mind, linked to instinct, animalistic urges, emotions and hidden memories.
Example: Eric's desire to force himself upon Eva Smith.

Superego—reality. This part of your mind makes decisions and controls your conscience, the difference between what is right and wrong. This operates on conscious and subconscious levels.
Example: The 'cold' Mrs Birling's superego dominates when she influences the charity committee not to help the pregnant, desperate Eva Smith.

Ego—morality. Also operating on conscious and subconscious levels, the ego is organised and realistic. It recognises that other people also have needs. It tries to meet the needs of the id and the superego.
Example: Sheila's id dominated when she became angry with Eva Smith at Milwards. Her superego dominated when she rationalised her anger by urging the manager at Milwards to fire Eva, or the Birlings would close their account. By the end of the play, her ego dominates when she regrets her actions 'I behaved badly too. I know I did. I'm ashamed of it'.

Feminist Interpretation

Important note: As was pointed out in the 2019 AQA report on the exam, critical theories should only be used in an exam answer if they enhance your interpretation of a text. You should not merely 'bolt on' comments about Marxism, Freud, feminism etc.

In 1792, Mary Wollstonecraft (mother of Mary Shelley, author of Frankenstein) published A Vindication of the Rights of Woman: with Strictures on Political and Moral Subjects. She challenged the contemporary view that women were weak, too full of emotions and not capable of 'rational' thought. She argued that girls should have the same education as boys. Wollstonecraft could be described as a proto-feminist, someone whose ideas were a forerunner of feminism—feminism as a concept did not exist before the twentieth century.

In the 1850s, the subject of women's rights became increasingly prominent as some women, particularly those in the higher social classes, refused to obey their male counterparts. New laws reveal the struggle of women to gain legal rights: in 1857, a divorced woman could sue an ex-husband and in 1882, a married woman finally had the legal right to own property.

Suffrage—the right to vote in political elections—also became increasingly prominent from the 1850s onwards. The militant suffragette movement fought for the right to vote, attracting significant news coverage until World War I. As we are aware (see character analysis of Edna), some women were given the vote in 1918, six years after the play is set. It was only in 1928 that all women could vote.

In 1949, journalist Simone de Beauvoir, published The Second Sex, which analysed how women were oppressed in society and helped to lay the foundation for the modern feminist movement. Key ideas are as follows:

- Women are 'the second sex' because they are regarded as less powerful and important than men.
- Gender is a social construction: society expects men and women to behave in particular ways.
- Society is patriarchal; in other words, it is dominated by men, who hold the power from which women are largely excluded.
- Women are restricted by their gender. They are valued:
    o For their looks.
    o For their ability to fulfil roles as wives and mothers.

A feminist might argue that:

- The plight of Eva Smith shows the danger men of in a patriarchal society holding a disproportionate amount of power.
- Both Gerald and Eric objectify women, commenting on Eva's looks, for which she is valued. They also comment on the appearances of the older prostitutes.
- When Gerald treats Eva as a commodity (a useful or valuable thing), he keeps her as his mistress for six months and then ends the relationship when it is no longer convenient.
- Eric has a sense of male entitlement when he sexually assaults Eva.
- Sheila in the opening stage directions is defined by her attractiveness to the opposite sex: she is a 'pretty girl'. Her engagement conforms to contemporary expectations in which she will become a wife and mother. Her evolving independence and confidence demonstrate how important it is to empower women. When she refuses to accept Gerald's ring at the end of the play, she realises that there is more to think about than marriage to Gerald.
- Mr Birling patronises women, calling Eva and her work colleagues 'girls', which belittles them.
- Mr and Mrs Birling both infantilise Sheila, calling her a 'girl' even though she is old enough to become engaged and marry.
- Sheila is seen to be delicate and in need of protection: Gerald wants her to leave the room before his confession. He does not, however, view Eva Smith in this way.
- Mrs Birling accepts her role in the patriarchal society by behaving in a subservient manner toward her husband.
- Mrs Birling accepts that women must come second to their husbands' work. She promotes the idea of female submission to Sheila, excusing Gerald's neglect: 'When you're married, you'll realise that men with important work to do sometimes have to spend nearly all their time and energy on their business'.
- Edna's silence symbolises the lack of power that women had in the 1912 patriarchy. Women could not vote, so had no political voice to influence how society was run.

Writing about the Play

First, you need to know which exam board you are on—your teacher will be able to answer this question. A summary of the boards and requirements for the response to 'An Inspector Calls' is below:

AQA: You will have a choice of two questions. You are required to write one essay.
Mark schemes: one mark scheme for the essay, plus four additional marks are available for written accuracy.

OCR: Two questions: (1) a response to an extract and (2) a response to a second question that links the character(s) or theme from the extract to the rest of the play.
Mark schemes: two separate mark schemes.

Pearson (Edexcel): You will have a choice of two questions. You are required to write one essay.
Mark schemes: one mark scheme for the essay, plus eight additional marks are available for written accuracy.

WJEC EDUQAS: Essay based on an extract from the play. In your essay, you are also expected to also talk about other parts of the play.
Mark schemes: one mark scheme for the essay, plus five additional marks are available for written accuracy.

In the Exam

The Question
Read the question carefully and underline the key words.

Thinking and Planning
1. Remember that you cannot write about everything that you have learnt. It is better to write a lot about a little (e.g. a detailed analysis of 5-6 quotes) rather than a little about a lot.
2. If your exam board provides you with an extract, annotate it, but only annotate what is relevant to the question. Then number which annotations you will write about, in order of importance.
3. Always plan your essay! If you are asked about a character (for example, Sheila), remember in your plan to show how her character changes throughout the play. Likewise, you have a thematic question, consider how that theme is developed throughout the play.
4. Plan to include a response to context. This response should show how context helps to inform your understanding. NB: You should know from earlier exam practice essays set by your English teacher how many marks are allocated to writing about context. It might be that you only need to write about it once.
5. Try and use short quotations if possible. Zoom in on words and phrases that Priestley has used. Analyse what they make you think or feel and imagine, explaining your reasons.
6. Remember to put single quotation marks around quotations (unless you are American, and you use what we call double speech marks).
7. Finally, prioritise your points: number them in the order that you are going to write about them. If you run out of time, you can drop the least important points.

Writing
1. Remember to always use the best, most formal vocabulary you can.
2. Keep your eye on the clock! If you run out of time, don't rush to cram in all your ideas. Focus on the most important points and develop your analysis. It is better to write a lot about a little than a little about a lot!

Checking
1. If marks are available for written accuracy, you should check your work carefully.
2. Check for other mistakes.

Example Essays
You are going to read two exam questions. Each question has three example essays (six essays in total).

The exemplar essays apply to your exam board in the following way:

AQA and Pearson (Edexcel): You are required to write one essay, so all of the example essays below are relevant.

OCR: Your response would be in two parts. Use the ideas in the essays that follow, but you would have to adapt them to an appropriate extract, followed by a separate response to the second question.

WJEC EDUQAS: You are required to write one essay, so all of the example essays below are relevant. The only difference is that your essay would be in response to an extract from the play.

Task
Read the three example exam essays that answer the same question. As you read, consult your mark scheme(s). Decide which mark(s) you would give each essay and why. The line spacing has been increased to make it easier for you to annotate.

Please note that the essays are not prescriptive: other students might choose different examples and gain the same mark...You can't write about everything!

How does Priestley deliver his Message of Social Responsibility in 'An Inspector Calls'?

Example Essay 1

'An Inspector Calls' is set in 1912, a time when there was a class divide in Britain and many were expected to know their place in society and not attempt to disrupt that position. Priestley's play was first performed in England in 1946, just as two World Wars had ended. An audience at the time had suffered the consequences of others refusing to take responsibility for their actions. It was also a time when bosses were most concerned with the profit, rather than the welfare of their workers. Through his play, it could be argued that Priestley delivers a message of social responsibility to an audience in the hope that they may realise the need to educate young people and have them think about the effect their actions may have on those they meet. As a socialist, Priestley believed that all citizens should be cared for; the focus should not just be on the wealthy few.

Inspector Goole appears to be the voice of Priestley in the play. He is the one who speaks to the Birling family about their alleged role in the death of Eva Smith. As he arrives on stage, the stage directions suggest a lighting change from 'pink and intimate' to 'brighter and harder'. Prior to the inspector's arrival, the 'pink and intimate' lighting suggests that the characters are looking at life through rose-tinted glasses. In other words, happy with their lives, they are oblivious to any wrongdoing. When the lighting changes to 'brighter and harder', it is as if the inspector has come to metaphorically shine a spotlight on the Birlings. His presence will shed light on the 'chain of events' which led to the death of Eva Smith. He is there to reveal their guilt and try to teach them the lesson of social responsibility.

Mr Birling is the first to be questioned by the inspector over his role in the death of Eva Smith, a former employee of his company, Birling and Co. He seems keen to hold positions of power (for example, his previous position of 'Lord Mayor'), but he does not seem willing to accept the responsibility which comes with such positions. The inspector is quick to remind him that 'Public men... have responsibilities as well as privileges'. This can also be seen as Priestley's view. Mr Birling is almost a caricature of a capitalist businessman. The playwright uses him to criticise others who hold similar positions in society.

Mr Birling is seen as an ultimately selfish man who is only concerned with the profit of his company. He voices opinions such as 'a man has to mind his own business and look after himself'. He even describes the idea of a more united society as 'community and all that nonsense', showing his unwillingness to take any responsibility for others. The structure of the play, however, serves in Priestley's favour as prior to these comments he has Mr Birling make other rash claims such as 'The Germans don't want war' and the Titanic is 'absolutely unsinkable'. An audience would know that not only did the Germans play a key part in World War II but the Titanic also sank. Priestley's effective use of dramatic irony here means Birling's opinions are instantly devalued. Priestley's clever structure means that when Birling follows these claims up with 'community and all that nonsense', we, the audience, may believe that he is continuing to talk rubbish. Priestley effectively gets the audience to agree with his own socialist views that community and taking responsibility for others is, in fact, far from 'nonsense'.

Society at the time failed to help or support Eva Smith and other girls like her. There was no Department for Work and Pensions or other welfare support. Priestley believed that we should all look after one another; his message is made clear in Inspector Goole's final speech. Firstly, Goole (or Priestley) makes it clear that Eva was not an isolated case. Eva Smith appears as a symbol for all women and men who are disadvantaged in society: 'One Eva Smith has gone – but there are millions and millions and millions of Eva Smiths and John Smiths still left with us'. The story has not finished with her death. There are other women and men (John Smiths) who need looking after. It is essential that we all take responsibility for our actions towards others, including those less fortunate than ourselves. 'Smith' is one of the most popular surnames in Britain, so this choice of name again highlights that there are many others out there, just like Eva, who need to be supported by their employers and other citizens.

This section of the inspector's final speech is followed by possibly the most important lines in the play: 'We don't live alone. We are members of one body. We are responsible for each other'. These effectively sum up Priestley's overall message.

The final part of the speech contains a warning for those unwilling to accept this lesson of social responsibility: there will be 'fire and blood and anguish'. The words 'fire and blood and anguish' have at least two possible interpretations. They closely resemble Hell imagery in the Bible and could suggest that if men and women are unwilling to take responsibility for one another here on earth, then they will be sent to Hell to learn the lesson there ('fire' and 'anguish' certainly suggest Hell). Alternatively, the phrase could refer to war since 'fire and blood and anguish' have connotations of war. Priestley, via the inspector, warns both the Birlings and an audience that if men and women refuse to look after one another, more wars may follow. The play was first performed just after the two world wars, but it was set in 1912, just before World War I. The Birlings who are from a society where many of the rich were selfish and only concerned with themselves and their money, would be just about to go through that war. Priestley/the inspector's words and warning are therefore highly relevant to both the characters and an audience.

To conclude, the inspector delivers Priestley's message about social responsibility.

Example Essay 2

The character of the inspector serves to deliver Priestley's message of social responsibility in 'An Inspector Calls'. We are first introduced to this idea through the stage directions and his name. When we meet Inspector Goole, he is described in the stage directions as creating an impression of 'massiveness, solidity and purposefulness'. The rule of three with the nouns creates a sense of his presence filling a room. He is therefore a catalyst who controls events through his questioning of characters. The words 'solidity and purposefulness' suggest that he has a purpose for his visit and that he cannot be persuaded to change his mind. Finally, his name is a homophone for ghoul, suggesting that he is interested in the dead, and this relates to the purpose of his visit. Goole is also a fishing village, which might imply that he is there to fish for information.

Throughout the play, Priestley uses Inspector Goole as his mouthpiece to deliver a message of social responsibility (socialism) to the audience. This is reflected in the instructions for lighting in the stage directions. As the inspector arrives, the stage directions propose a lighting change from 'pink and intimate' to 'brighter and harder'. Prior to the inspector's arrival, the 'pink and intimate' lighting symbolises that the characters are looking at life through rose-tinted spectacles. In other words, they are oblivious to any wrongdoing, and they are happy with their lives. When the lighting changes to 'brighter and harder', it is as if the inspector has come to metaphorically shine a spotlight on the Birlings; this has connotations of a harsh interrogation light from which they cannot escape. The inspector is there to reveal the characters' guilt about the death of Eva Smith and to try to teach them a lesson of social responsibility. It is implied therefore through the lighting that the characters (and by default, the audience) cannot escape the message of socialism.

In addition, sound effects are used to convey Priestley's message of socialism. For example, when Mr Birling is expressing his capitalist views to his family ('a man has to mind his own business'), he is interrupted by the 'sharp ring' of the doorbell. This suggests that the inspector is there to challenge Mr Birling's views. The adjective 'sharp' also connotes pain, foreshadowing that the Inspector will be harsh towards the family and Gerald Croft, and judgemental of their capitalist views.

The inspector's final speech sums up Priestley's overall message about socialism: 'We don't live alone. We are members of one body. We are responsible for each other'. The play is set in 1912, and he makes predictions that the audience, who has lived through two world wars, will know are true: there will be 'fire and blood and anguish'. The words 'fire and blood and anguish' have at least two possible interpretations. Firstly, 'fire' and 'anguish' suggest Hell. These words closely resemble Biblical descriptions of Hell, and could suggest that if people are unwilling to take responsibility for one another here on earth, then they will be sent to Hell to learn the lesson there. Secondly, the words have connotations of war. Priestley, via the inspector, warns both the Birlings and the audience that if people refuse to look after one another, more wars may follow. Priestley/the inspector's warning are therefore highly relevant to both the characters (who will live through wars) and the audience.

Priestley contrasts the inspector's predictions with those of Mr Birling to emphasise that capitalism is wrong and socialism is right. For example, Mr Birling predicts that The Titanic is 'unsinkable', which is dramatic irony because the audience knows that the prediction—as well as his other predictions—is wrong. Through dramatic irony, the audience is encouraged to mistrust Birling's opinion of capitalism and therefore agree with the inspector's opinion of socialism, as the latter's predictions turn out to be correct.

The inspector is not meant to be a real person at all: in the play, we see that his ideas are what are important, and the younger generation understands this. Sheila and Eric are still upset at the end of the play, regardless of whether anyone actually died or if the inspector was actually real. Priestley ensures that all audience members realise the impact of his message by adding the final phone call at the very end of the play. The phone rings 'sharply' like the doorbell and the characters learn that a girl has now died. This suggests that what Goole said in his final speech is true—that men and women will be forced to learn the lesson of social responsibility one way or another. It is inescapable.

To conclude, the message of the play could still be seen as relevant today, as the poor are still with us, not just within the UK but in the world. Even though in the UK we now have social benefits, a welfare state, charities and unions, some difficulties remain when members of society act in selfish way or are unwilling to help one another. In many ways, Priestley's message of social responsibility in 'An Inspector Calls' could therefore be said to be as relevant today as when it was first performed in England in 1945.

Example Essay 3

Priestley uses the character of Inspector Goole to deliver his anti-capitalist message of social responsibility in 'An Inspector Calls'.

The inspector is a mouthpiece for Priestley's message, and he is not intended to represent a real person. We first learn this through the stage directions in which the inspector creates 'an impression of massiveness, solidity and purposefulness'. The triadic list of nouns helps us to focus on his personal qualities. The abstract noun 'massiveness' creates a sense that the inspector's presence metaphorically fills the room, almost as if he is a supernatural presence. The word 'solidity' can be used to describe a strong or firm structure; it is also used to describe a reliable person. Both interpretations have positive connotations and create the impression that the inspector has good, solid, reliable views, upon which the audience (and by default, society) can depend. The last word in the list, 'purposefulness' connotes determination: the inspector is there for a reason, and nothing will stop him from spreading Priestley's socialist message. The three nouns therefore combine to depict the inspector as a strong character who will use the force of his personality to challenge the capitalist views of the Birlings and Gerald Croft. Furthermore, Priestley writes that the inspector creates 'an impression of' these qualities, suggesting an other-worldly element to his personality. If we view the inspector through the lens of Freud's dreams theory, a psychoanalytical interpretation might be that the inspector is in fact a manifestation of the characters' inner guilt. This implies that, even before the play began, the characters felt some subconscious guilt about their treatment of Eva Smith. I am not entirely sure that I agree with this interpretation because there is no evidence for this in the play; but the announcement at the end of the play that another inspector is on his way might lend Freud's dreams theory more credibility as, by the end of the play, all the characters have been given the opportunity to examine their consciences.

Priestley also uses elements of Aristotle's Three Unities of drama to help the audience to focus on the inspector's socialist message: 'We don't live alone. We are members of one body. We are responsible for each other'. Firstly, the play conforms to the Unity of Time, as all the events in the play (stage time) happen in real time. The audience experiences events unfolding at the same time as the characters. This helps to hammer home Priestley's socialist message, enforced above with the triad of simple sentences and the use of anaphora with 'we' to emphasise that we are part of the collective body of the human race. Priestley adheres to the Unity of Place with the single setting of the Birlings' dining-room; without the distraction of other settings, the attention of the audience is focused more fully on Priestley's message. Finally, until the inspector's exit, Priestley adheres to the final unity, Unity of Action, in which there is just one main storyline, driven by the inspector's questions about their role in the death of Eva Smith. This makes the play easier for the audience to follow, and they are more likely to reflect on the ideas within the play. In a sense, the inspector also assumes the role of the Greek Chorus in Classical Greek drama. As Priestley's mouthpiece, he summarises the 'chain of events' surrounding Eva's life, comments on the characters' behaviour and, with his exit speech, explains what lesson they need to learn.

After the inspector exits, the focus of the play changes to the debate about whether the inspector is a real police inspector but Priestley, through Sheila and Eric, emphasises that this does not matter, as his message of social responsibility is more important. Sheila, perhaps picking up the mantle of the inspector's role of Greek Chorus, repeats the inspector's words of 'Fire and blood and anguish' from his exit speech. Priestley employs syndetic listing to slow down the pace and allow each word in the list to have a greater impact on the audience. The playwright might be alluding to the Biblical description of Hell being a 'blazing furnace, where there will be weeping and gnashing of teeth' as a warning that if people do not embrace his socialist message, they are destined to go to Hell. The Biblical language adds to the supernatural, other-worldly aspect of inspector Goole, which helps us to remember his message. This imagery of 'fire and blood and anguish' can also be interpreted as foreshadowing the pain and suffering of the two world wars which would soon follow the historical setting of the play. The contemporary audience would be fully aware of the 'fire and blood and anguish' of WW1 and WW2, so this adds to the sense of mystery surrounding Goole: how exactly does he know so clearly what is to follow? Knowing that Goole is right adds credibility to his ideas about socialism, just as knowing Birling is wrong about the 'unsinkable' Titanic and the Germans not wanting war being used to undermine his capitalist agenda. Sheila repeating the inspector's words shows that she has learnt her lesson, and this also reinforces the inspector's message of social responsibility.

Priestley ensures that all audience members realise the impact of the inspector's message with the stage direction of the final phone call at the end of the play. The phone rings 'sharply', echoing the 'sharp ring' of the doorbell that had first accompanied the arrival of the inspector. Both sound effects interrupt Mr Birling expressing his views, almost personifying the doorbell and then the phone, suggesting that they sharply disagree with his views. By ending a play on a moment of high tension when we hear that a young woman has died and an inspector is on his way, Priestley leaves the audience with the suggestion that what Goole said in his final speech is true: the Birlings and Gerald cannot escape learning their lesson of social responsibility. Priestley himself studied the concept of time and Dunne's theory, which focuses on learning from mistakes. Dunne proposes that we have all been given the ability to look forward in time so that we can avoid errors before we make them (as well as learning from mistakes in our past). Perhaps the pending arrival of a real inspector at the end of the play is therefore an opportunity for the older Birlings and Croft to examine their consciences once more and learn from their mistakes of the past.

To conclude, Priestley deliberately surrounds the character of Inspector Goole with an air of mystery in order to encourage the audience to concentrate on his words. His message of social responsibility ('We are members of one body. We are responsible for each other') eclipses all other ideas in the play. By ending the play with a twist, Priestley encourages the audience to discuss the play, particularly the character of the inspector, and take his message of social responsibility home with them.

How does Priestley present the Differences between the older and younger Generations of the Birling Family in 'An Inspector Calls'?

Example Essay 1

Mr Birling is first introduced in the play as a 'heavy-looking, rather portentous man in his middle fifties with fairly easy manners but rather provincial in his speech'. Our immediate impression of him is as a person who is rather self-centred and confident, a man who is proud of his standing in society. He frequently reminds everyone of his achievements of being a 'Lord Mayor' and his hope for a 'knighthood'. Priestley presents us with little to like about Mr Birling from the start. The playwright uses him as a symbol of the capitalist society which Priestley, being a socialist, was against.

Sheila is Mr Birling's daughter who, at the start of the play, has just become engaged to Gerald Croft. During the early 1900s when the play is set, women were seen chiefly as the possession of their fathers or husbands. Sheila is a symbol of the younger generation of wealthy members of society. Priestley uses her and her brother Eric to demonstrate that younger people can be taught the lesson of social responsibility.

At the start of the play, just as her father is concerned with accolades and public recognition, so Sheila seems concerned with her appearance and material goods. Despite getting engaged to Gerald, it is only when he gives her the ring that she says she can really 'feel engaged'. Our impression is of a young, somewhat naïve girl who is rather superficial and certainly unaware of how her treatment of others could have an effect on their lives. It is not until the inspector points out her involvement with Eva Smith that Sheila has any recollection of her encounter with her at Milwards. Similarly, Mr Birling needs reminding that Eva Smith worked for his company before he sacked her for campaigning for better wages.

Mr Birling is happy about the engagement of Sheila to Gerald Croft, not because he believes they love each other and will make each other happy, more because by marrying Gerald, Sheila will increase her social status. Gerald is a man whose parents own an even more successful company than Birling and Co. Mr Birling says hopes that one day the Crofts and Birlings will be 'working together—for lower costs and higher prices.' Mr Birling presents the union almost as a business deal and he makes it clear that 'a man has to mind his own business and look after himself'. Mr Birling seems concerned that he does not have the same kind of family connections that Gerald has; he has to rely on money he has made rather than that which has been passed on to him. His mention of a knighthood is significant, as this is an award given as recognition for services to the community. J.B. Priestley again seems to be criticising Mr Birling and his actions as we later find that he does not support the notion of community at all.

At the start of the play, Mr Birling makes claims such as 'The Germans don't want war' and that the Titanic is 'absolutely unsinkable'. The audience knew that the Germans played a key part in World War II, and the Titanic also sank. Priestley's effective use of dramatic irony here means Birling's opinions are instantly devalued. Priestley's clever structure means that when Birling follows this up with 'community and all that nonsense', we, the audience, may believe that he is continuing to talk rubbish. Priestley effectively uses this structure to encourage his audiences to agree with his own socialist views that community is, in fact, far from 'nonsense'.

Mr Birling sacked Eva Smith because she demanded a higher (and probably fairer) wage and went on strike: 'She'd had a lot to say—far too much—so she had to go'. The play is set at a time when many workers were going on strike for better pay and conditions. Mr Birling's lack of regret over his actions means that it is hard to sympathise with him.

Following Mr Birling's interrogation, Sheila said she was shopping at Milwards when she first met Eva. Sheila believed a dress looked better against Eva. Her jealousy led to her using her influence as a valued customer to have Eva sacked, saying she would 'persuade mother to close our account'. Sheila now realises the enormity of the situation she does become very distressed; the stage directions say how she looks 'as if she's been crying', which shows she regrets her actions ('I behaved badly too. I know I did. I'm ashamed of it'). Priestley uses her to demonstrate that young people can learn the lesson of social responsibility. There is therefore hope for the future of society if we can make them realise the need to look after others they come into contact with, even if those other people are of a lower social status than themselves.

Mr Birling, however, does not show the same morals and capability to learn the lesson of social responsibility. Priestley uses him to represent the older generation who are more inclined to be set in their ways. Mr Birling does not admit that he was in any way to blame for the death of Eva Smith and, even after other characters such as Sheila and Eric have broken down and clearly been sorry for their actions, Mr Birling insists, 'I can't accept any responsibility'. He fails to learn the inspector (and Priestley's) lesson of social responsibility which supports the idea that it is the younger members of society who need to be educated and encouraged to look out for one another if society is to become a better place.

The audience are likely to leave with the view that, even if you try to ignore your responsibilities, just as Mr Birling did, your actions will eventually be punished. Sheila (and her brother Eric) accepting responsibility for their actions effectively shows the audience that there is hope for the future; if we educate young people, then they can learn to take responsibility for each other and make a better society for everyone to live in.

Example Essay 2

In this essay, I will discuss the characters of Mr Birling to represent the older generation and Sheila Birling to represent the younger generation. Both characters are used by Priestley to convey his views about capitalism and socialism.

Firstly, Priestley uses Mr Birling as a symbol of the capitalistic society which Priestley, being a socialist, was against. Mr Birling is first introduced in the play as a 'heavy-looking, rather portentous man in his middle fifties'. The adjective 'heavy' suggests that he will not move easily from his point of view. The second adjective 'portentous' implies that he is rather self-centred and confident; he will not readily listen to the views of others. Furthermore, his age suggests that he is fixed in his views. Priestley presents through the stage directions a character who is entrenched in his views and is not very likeable. This will prejudice the audience them against him.

Priestley also employs dramatic irony to show that Mr. Birling's capitalist views are wrong. Mr Birling makes predictions such as 'The Germans don't want war' and the Titanic is 'unsinkable'. The play is set in 1912 so, by making these comments, the 1945 Soviet audiences and 1946 British audiences know that the Germans played a key part in World War II and that the Titanic sank on her maiden voyage. Priestley's use of dramatic irony means that Birling's capitalist opinions that follow are instantly worthless. The playwright's clever structure means that when Birling talks about 'community and all that nonsense', the audience is encouraged to believe that his views are wrong. Priestley therefore uses this structure to encourage the audience to agree with his own socialist views that community is, in fact, far from 'nonsense'.

Mr. Birling could be seen as a caricature of a typical capitalist businessman of the time, heartless and ruthless, concerned only with himself and his wealth. The play is set at a time when many workers were going on strike for better pay and conditions, as trade unions were in their infancy. It is ironic that he sacked Eva for being a ringleader in the strike ('She'd had a lot to say—far too much—so she had to go'), as he had previously intended to promote her for showing the same leadership skills. The short phrases separated by hyphens suggest a contemptuous, dismissive attitude and that he sacked her with little thought despite her hard work. Mr. Birling's lack of regret over his actions ('I can't accept any responsibility') means that it is hard for the audience to sympathise with him.

In contrast, Priestley uses Sheila to demonstrate that younger people can be taught the lesson of social responsibility. During the early 1900s when the play is set, women were seen chiefly regarded as the possession of their fathers or husbands so, at the start of the play, we do not see Sheila as responsible for anything. She does not seem to have a job, and she is dependent on her family's account when she goes shopping at Milwards. Sheila seems concerned with her appearance and material goods. Despite getting engaged to Gerald, it is only when he gives her the ring that she says she can really 'feel engaged'. Our impression is of a young, somewhat naïve girl, who is rather superficial and is unaware of how her treatment of others could have an effect on their lives. It is not until the inspector points out her involvement with Eva Smith that Sheila remembers her encounter with her at Milwards. (Similarly, Mr. Birling needs reminding that Eva Smith worked for his company before he sacked her for campaigning for better wages.)

Unlike Mr Birling, Sheila realises the enormity of being responsible for the sacking of Eva Smith, and Priestley uses stage directions to show her distress: she looks 'as if she's been crying'. These stage directions are to encourage the audience to note how sorry she is for what she has done and to conclude that she has changed. Sheila clearly regrets her actions: 'I behaved badly too. I know I did. I'm ashamed of it'. The rule of three with the simple sentences indicates that her regret is genuine. Priestley uses the character of Sheila to demonstrate that young people can learn the lesson of social responsibility. There is therefore hope for the future of society if we can make them realise the need to look after others.

The theme of the younger generation being able to change is developed through the character of Sheila, who is the product of her environment. Being brought up in a wealthy family in Edwardian England means that she has probably had little responsibility for her actions until this point, rather like a child. She seems to grow in confidence as the play progresses, however. At the start of the play, she calls Mrs Birling 'mummy' and at the end she calls her 'mother'; the change from the childish to adult term of address symbolises that she has grown and matured. She also refuses to take back the engagement ring when she finds out Gerald has cheated on her saying, 'it's too soon'. This shows her increased strength and ability to make morally sound decisions on her own, rather than being dominated by the men in her life. This might reflect the growing suffragette movement of the time in which women of all classes, campaigning for the vote, were demanding the right to have their say in how the country was run.

To conclude, the audience is likely to leave the theatre with the view that even if you try to ignore your responsibilities, just as Mr Birling does, your actions will eventually be punished (the 'fire and blood and anguish' of the inspector's predications might link to the world wars but they might also connote the pains of Hell). In contrast, Sheila accepting responsibility for her actions shows the audience that there is hope for the future: if we educate young people, they can learn to take responsibility for each other and create a better society for everyone to live in.

Example Essay 3
Priestley uses the older generation of the Birling family to illustrate that, in the playwright's opinion, the older generation are fixed in their capitalist ways and will not change. In contrast, he uses the younger generation as a symbol of hope: they are open to new ideas and are more willing to embrace Priestley's socialist message: 'We don't live alone. We are members of one body. We are responsible for each other'. This essay will explore key ideas to do with the older and younger generation, focusing on the characters of Mr Birling and Sheila.

Priestley depicts Mr. Birling is a caricature of a capitalist businessman of the time, heartless and ruthless, concerned only with himself and his wealth. From a Marxist perspective, Mr Birling with his focus on 'lower costs and higher prices' symbolises the capitalist exploiter of the proletariat, who are valued only for their labour. Before the arrival of the inspector, he declares 'a man has to mind his own business and look after himself and his own'. This statement aligns him with making money ('business') which is then juxtaposed with his own needs ('look after himself'). It is almost as if he is so selfish that the reference to his family ('and his own') comes as an afterthought. This view is challenged by Priestley with the 'sharp ring' of the door bell. The use of the adjective 'sharp' implies that Mr Birling has violated the laws of humanity to the extent that even inanimate objects disagree with him. Priestley, being a socialist, shows no mercy towards Mr Birling; undoubtedly, there were men like Mr Birling, but the playwright completely ignores the historical backdrop of rich philanthropic Victorian industrialists who showed corporate social responsibility. For example, Sir

Titus Salt, Rowntree, the Cadbury brothers and the Lever Brothers, who built a model villages for their workforces, with decent housing, gardens, parks and other amenities. Perhaps Priestley's bias is because the play contains elements of a morality play that aims to teach people lessons about how to behave. Mr Birling's character might be the personification of the Deadly Sin of Avarice. Priestley expects the audience to learn a moral message from about social responsibility from the play, and it is much easier to stand back and judge a two-dimensional stereotype than a more realistic person with depth and complications.

Priestley also employs dramatic irony to show the audience that they cannot trust Mr Birling's opinions. For example, the 1912 Mr Birling makes a range of predictions, which the original audiences (the 1945 Soviet audiences and 1946 British audiences) knew were wrong. One of these predictions is that the Titanic is 'absolutely unsinkable'. The adverb 'absolutely' emphasises Mr Birling's conviction that he is right—but the Titanic sank on its maiden voyage in 15th April, 1912, not long after the play is set. Perhaps Priestley includes the Titanic example as a metaphor for Edwardian society. The ship had First Class, Second Class and Third Class passengers, whose accommodation was on allocated decks. This might represent the class structure of Edwardian society and Priestley's view that the rich First Class passengers chose to detach themselves completely from their poorer counterparts. Interestingly, a Grand Staircase connected the ship's seven decks. This might symbolise the inspector's words that 'We are members of one body', connected to each other, whether we like it or not. Furthermore, the ship only had twenty lifeboats, which were not enough for the 3,300 passengers and crew. This appalling planning might symbolise the complacency of people like Mr Birling, who are overconfident in their views. Finally, the sinking of the Titanic might represent the sinking of Edwardian society in which attitudes were being challenged by Priestley and his writer friends such as George Bernard Shaw and HG Wells, and in which World War I would change attitudes to class. Priestley's use of this and other examples of dramatic irony encourages the audience to mistrust Mr Birling's views, particularly his views on capitalism and social responsibility.

In contrast, Priestley uses Sheila to demonstrate that younger people, particularly young women, can change and learn his lesson of social responsibility. A feminist literary critic might argue that, when in the opening stage directions she is described as a 'pretty girl', Sheila is defined by her attractiveness to the opposite sex. A Freudian interpretation might be that Sheila's id dominated her base instincts of jealousy and anger about Eva being more attractive than her when she held the dress against herself. Sheila's superego then dominated her id as she rationalised her anger and said that she would 'persuade mother to close our account' if Milwards did not fire Eva. After the inspector's interrogation, Sheila has completely changed her views. Her ego now dominates when she regrets her actions: 'I behaved badly too. I know I did. I'm ashamed of it'. Priestley's triad of simple sentences forces the audience to follow her words closely and to appreciate that her regret is genuine.

Feeling sorry for Eva Smith is one thing but having the power to change into a better person is another, but Priestley suggests that this is possible. Feminist Simone de Beauvoir states in The Second Sex that women are restricted by their gender. We have already seen how Sheila being valued for her looks might affects her behaviour. Beauvoir also asserts that women are valued for their ability to fulfil roles as wives and mothers. At the beginning of the play, Sheila's engagement conforms to contemporary expectations. She also accepts a subordinate role to Gerald, asking him 'is it the one you wanted me to have?'. Priestley's use of the interrogative shows that she is happy to accept a passive role in which she has no say about a ring that she, at this point in the play, intends to wear for the rest of her life. In 1912, women were regarded as inferior to men (Beauvoir's 'second sex'). Priestley suggests that socialism improves women like Sheila when, at the end of the play, she refuses to take back the engagement ring, saying 'It's too soon. I must think'. Her use of simple declarative sentences emphasises a strength of character that was not present at the beginning of the play. She is now a confident young woman, aware that she has more options in life than marriage. Priestley's use of the modal verb 'must' shows that it is imperative, an obligation, that she consider her future. She will not be hurried into making decisions and needs time to consider her options. <u>She</u> makes the decisions—not Gerald. In fact, in the Soviet Union, in 1918, Lenin later stated: 'The status of women up to now has been compared to that of a slave; women have been tied to the home, and only socialism can save them from this'. Sheila's evolving independence and confidence therefore demonstrates how important socialism appears to be for the empowerment of women.

To conclude, the audience is likely to view the younger generation of the Birling family in a more positive way than the older generation. Sheila accepting responsibility for her actions shows the audience that there is hope for Priestley's socialist message: if we educate all young people, including women, they will embrace the playwright's socialist message and create a better society for everyone. We must also not forget that, when the play was first performed, the audience members had just experienced World War II, so they would probably be keen to see a more compassionate society in which people take responsibility for their actions.

Key Quotations

Quote	Character	Theme/comment
'pink and intimate'	Lighting Birling family	At the start of the play, this stage direction suggests the Birlings have an overly optimistic view of life.
'brighter and harder'	Lighting Inspector	This stage direction suggests the inspector has arrived to shed light on the events. It connotes (1) an interrogation light and (2) a spotlight.
'heavily comfortable but not cosy and homelike'	Stage directions	Description of Birlings' house and furniture. Oxymoron and language analysis opportunity.
'port' 'cigar box' 'champagne glasses'	Stage directions	Description of Birlings' house and contents. Introduction of ideas to do with social class, wealth and self-indulgence.
'pleased with themselves'	Birling family Stage directions	How the Birling family are described at the start of the play.
'heavy-looking, rather portentous man in his middle fifties with fairly easy manners but rather provincial in his speech.'	Mr Birling	At the start of the play this description suggests Mr Birling is self-important, fixed in his views and has worked his way up.
'working together—for lower costs and higher prices'	Mr Birling	Mr Birling is pleased Sheila is engaged to Gerald but for business opportunities rather than love.
'a man has to mind his own business and look after himself and his own'	Mr Birling	Mr Birling's selfish, capitalist views at the start of the play.
'community and all that nonsense'	Mr Birling	Mr Birling's views on community at the start of the play.
'The Germans don't want war'	Mr Birling	Priestley uses dramatic irony to discredit Mr Birling's incorrect prediction.
'absolutely unsinkable'	Mr Birling	An incorrect prediction about the Titanic to make the audience mistrust Birling's opinions on other issues such as capitalism and socialism.
'behindhand'	Mr Birling	Dramatic irony: an incorrect prediction about the Soviet Union (which he calls Russia).
'Lord Mayor' 'knighthood'	Mr Birling	Shows he is concerned with his social status when he brags to Gerald.

Quote	Speaker	Explanation
'sound useful party man'	Mr Birling to Gerald	This is his reason for thinking he will get a knighthood: cash for honours, which today is illegal.
'I was an alderman for years—and I'm still on the Bench'	Mr Birling	Mr Birling reminds us of his position to try and exert authority over the Inspector.
'She'd had a lot to say—far too much—so she had to go'	Mr Birling about Eva	Mr Birling explains that he sacked Eva for voicing her opinions and striking over wages.
'I can't accept any responsibility'	Mr Birling	He refuses to accept any responsibility for his actions.
'Thousands'	Mr Birling	Worried about a scandal, Mr Birling says he will pay 'thousands' to put things right. He will pay money to save is reputation but not to give his employees a pay rise.
'But the whole thing's different now.'	Mr Birling	He thinks that if the inspector is not real and a girl didn't die then his actions don't matter.
'crank'	Mr Birling about the inspector	After he has left, Mr Birling tries to dismiss the inspector, aligning him with socialist sympathisers or cranks.
'cold' 'social superior' of Mr Birling	Mrs Birling	Stage directions: the words introduce the theme of class snobbery and lack of compassion for those who need it.
'prejudiced' 'girls of that class'	Mrs Birling	She admits to being 'prejudiced' against Eva. Feels contempt towards the working class.
'I told him quite plainly that I thought I had done no more than my duty.'	Mrs Birling	Mrs Birling refuses to feel guilty for her involvement.
'Go and look for the father of the child. It's his responsibility'	Mrs Birling	Mrs Birling unknowingly blames her son Eric, who had actually got Eva pregnant. Dramatic irony and very exciting for the audience, as she sets herself up.
'I did nothing that I'm ashamed of'	Mrs Birling	Refuses to accept any responsibility for her actions.
'pretty girl in her early twenties, very pleased with life and rather excited'	Sheila	Stage directions: description of Sheila, a young woman who is infantilised.
'Is it the one you wanted me to have?'	Sheila to Gerald	She accepts a subordinate role: he is the decision maker about her engagement ring.

'feel engaged'	Sheila	Sheila needs the engagement ring before she says she can really 'feel engaged'. She appears to be rather superficial.
'last summer, when you never came near me, and I wondered what had happened to you'	Sheila about Gerald	Sheila first raises suspicion about Gerald's actions near the start of the play. This hints at underlying tension. NB: She does not challenge him.
'persuade mother to close our account'	Sheila	She threatened to 'persuade mother to close our account' at Milwards if the manager did not sack Eva.
'as if she's been crying'	Sheila Stage direction	Sheila is visibly upset about her involvement in the chain of events leading to Eva's death.
'I behaved badly too. I know I did. I'm ashamed of it'	Sheila	Sheila accepts responsibility for her actions.
'he knows. Of course he knows'	Sheila to Gerald	Sheila's recognition that the inspector already knows everything about their involvement with the chain of events, so there is no point lying or withholding any information.
'wonderful fairy prince'	Sheila to Gerald	Sarcasm as she asserts herself.
'It's too soon. I must think.'	Sheila	Sheila refuses to take back the engagement ring from Gerald at the end of the play. She has changed and realises that there are more options for the future than traditional marriage and children.
'Half shy, half assertive'	Eric Birling	Immature. '[S]hy' implies secrets. Do we trust him? '[A]ssertive' foreshadows him forcing himself on Eva. Unformed as a character, so there is potential to change.
'squiffy'	Eric	The word used to describe Eric's drunkenness.
'sneak'	Eric to Sheila	Eric briefly turns against Sheila as she reveals details of his drinking.
'you know'	Eric	Eric realises that the inspector already knows the truth about his involvement.
'in that state when a chap easily turns nasty'	Eric	Eric describing his behaviour when he went to Eva's lodgings and insisted that she let him in.
'And that's when it happened. And I don't even remember—that's the hellish thing.'	Eric	Eric vaguely describes how he forced himself on Eva.

Quote	Character	Explanation
'not a kind of father a chap could go to when he's in trouble'	Eric to Mr Birling	Eric describes his distant relationship with his father.
'you turned her away—yes, and you killed her'	Eric to Mrs Birling	Eric blames his mother for what happened.
'It's what happened to the girl and what we all did to her that matters'	Eric	Eric realises that they must all accept responsibility.
'We did her in all right.'	Eric	Eric is frustrated at his parents' refusal to admit their wrongdoings.
'We often do on the young ones. They're more impressionable.'	Inspector	The inspector explains that young people can be taught to take responsibility for others.
'easy, well-bred young man-about-town'	Gerald	Opening stage directions focus on his social status and worldly experience.
'politely'	Gerald, agreeing with Mr Birling	Like Mrs Birling, Gerald is aware that Mr Birling should not compliment a servant. The stage direction 'politely' shows Gerald's good manners and diplomacy.
'Very pretty—soft brown hair and big dark eyes'	Gerald about Eva Smith	She is vulnerable...and he judges her by her looks.
'I don't come into this suicide business.'	Gerald	Gerald initially refuses to admit any wrongdoing.
'Well?'	Inspector to Gerald	Only the one word is needed from the inspector for Gerald to realise the need to tell his story. Ends Act 1 on a moment of suspense, as the tension rises.
'She didn't blame me at all. I wish to God she had now.'	Gerald	Gerald does take some responsibility for his actions.
'Everything's alright now.'	Gerald	When he thinks the inspector might be fake, Gerald thinks the issue has been resolved.
'sharp ring'	Stage direction	The doorbell announces the arrival of the inspector, interrupting Mr Birling expressing his capitalist opinions.
'an impression of massiveness, solidity and purposefulness'	Inspector	The inspector is described as a powerful man.
'burnt her inside out'	Inspector	Direct, shocking language used by the inspector to describe Eva's death.
'Chain of events'	Inspector	The inspector is a catalyst, questioning the characters, one at a time. The audience sees that they are all part of a chain of events, collectively responsible for Eva's death.

'few friends, lonely, half-starved' and 'desperate'	Inspector about Eva Smith	Priestley's deliberate use of emotive language to gain sympathy from the audience.
'Public men…have responsibilities as well as privileges'	Inspector Goole to Mr Birling	The inspector (as the voice of Priestley) reminds Mr Birling of his need to use his position in society to help others.
'One Eva Smith has gone—but there are millions and millions and millions of Eva Smiths and John Smiths still left with us'	Inspector (final speech)	In his final speech, the inspector reminds us this was not an isolated case. There are other men and women in society who need help.
'We don't live alone. We are members of one body. We are responsible for each other.'	Inspector (final speech)	The main message of the play—we must take responsibility for one another.
'fire and blood and anguish'	Inspector (final speech) Sheila	Goole explains that the lesson of social responsibility is unavoidable. If people do not choose to learn it, they will be made to on earth (in war) or in the afterlife (Hell). Sheila repeats these words at the end of the play, suggesting that she has taken on the inspector's role.
'rings sharply'	Stage direction	The telephone ringing at the end of the play mirrors the ringing of the doorbell at the beginning. Both sound effects herald the arrival of an inspector.

Printed in Great Britain
by Amazon